Covered In Pet Fur

How to Start an Animal Rescue the Right Way

Stacey Ritz & Amy Beatty

ROCKVILLE
PUBLISHING

Covered in Pet Fur: How to Start an Animal Rescue, The Right Way.

Stacey Ritz and Amy Beatty.

Published by Rockville Publishing

Front cover photo courtesy of Advocates 4 Animals, Inc.

Back cover photo courtesy of GCPS

ISBN: 978-1507557273

PRINTED IN THE UNITED STATES OF AMERICA

COVERED IN PET FUR

FORWARD

————

IT SAT IN A FORGOTTEN PART OF THE CITY. The dilapidated building was dark and surrounded by an eight foot tall barbed wire fence. The only sign was no larger than a sheet of computer paper. It was crookedly suspended, hanging from one rotting corner just above the padlock. It read "OPEN HOURS" and any remaining words had been long since bleached by the relentless sun. I double checked the address on my sheet of paper. (This was before I owned a cell phone and I had never dreamed that one day we would have GPS systems leading us anywhere we desired to go.) It was the correct address. But weren't animal shelters friendly places filled with

————

people who adored animals? Weren't non-profit organizations clean and welcoming? Weren't they there to help? My mind buzzed with questions, although neither of us said a word. We were still in undergraduate school learning the ways of the world. Yet we had no idea we were about to embark on one of our most impactful lessons as we hesitantly approached the padlocked gates.

A burley man in a blue and black checkered flannel vest strolled out to the fence from inside, a worn cigarette hanging from the left corner of his mouth as a cloud of smoke surrounded his solemn face. I admit I wanted to turn and run back to the safety of our car. But my curiosity got the best of me. Or maybe we were both just paralyzed; in shock from our new surroundings. We were accustomed to our plush college campus, bright lights, clean sidewalks, smiling faces...but somehow we had driven just a few miles away into what felt like the Twilight Zone. Maybe now, well over a decade later, I would have turned and run. No seriously, who I am kidding? I would have stayed. I wanted to know what was behind the barbed wire. I wanted to know what happened to the animals who were found being abused, who were no longer wanted through no fault of their own. I wanted to know the reality of life for companion animals in our country. And although we spent years volunteering at various shelters, pounds and sanctuaries around the Midwest, I attribute what we have built today to our first day at this particular shelter; where countless lives were tossed into the dark and left, forgotten by the rest of the world. *Out of sight, out of mind.*

We located the shelter address through the phone book. I am well aware that this dates us, as we were living in a pre-Google time. But maybe what saved us was my chatter. I'll never be sure, but back in those days I tended to ramble when my nerves got the best of me. It was my way of trying to calm myself. Whatever it was, the flannelled man we came to know as Todd pulled out his key and allowed us through the gates and into the city shelter. Our bewildered faces tried to take it all in. When we explained that we wanted to volunteer, Todd raised his eyebrows as if to indicate that we were crazy. He explained that he did not have any open paid positions, not understanding why anyone would subject themselves to this environment without receiving a paycheck. We told him we just wanted to spend time with the animals, to bring in toys for the cats, to take the dogs on walks; we just wanted to give them some love and attention while they waited behind bars for a slim chance at finding a home. Todd nodded, clearly thinking we would never return.

First, Todd led us to a narrow building they called "the cat room". Small rusty wire cages lined the room from floor to ceiling and stacked side by side. Only a slender opening existed down the center of the piles of cages leaving a space for us to walk. Cats received no vetting – no spay or neuter surgeries and certainly no vaccinations. A few animals had food in their cages, hardly any had water and the bowls looked as if they had been dry for quite some time. No one had toys and most of the litter boxes were overflowing with old feces. Many cats started meowing when we entered the room, some stuck their paws through the wire bars, begging for help. My initial reaction was to run and open every cage door and let them all run free in the room while we cleaned their cages and filled their bowls with fresh food and water. But instead I pressed my hands behind my back and tried to remain calm. We asked questions about how many adoptions occurred, why the cats in their care received absolutely no vetting and we learned that there had never been volunteers. *Never.*

Next we walked over to the main building. The room looked dilapidated and the small space was dark. No natural light existed. It looked more like an old barn than a shelter. There was no heating or air conditioning, just cages stacked in endless rows, filled with dogs of every color and size. Most of them couldn't stand up in their cages without having to hunch down in their cramped quarters. The dogs never left their crates unless by some odd stroke of luck a rare visitor adopted them. Todd said the only other way the dogs ever left their cages was if they died in their crates, and that happened too often. There were six long rows of wire dog crates lining what we grew to call The Warehouse. The crates were stacked on top of each other, just as the cats had been. Only with the dogs, some small dogs sat next to large dogs and they fought viciously through the bent metal bars, frustrated by their helpless fates. It was enough to rattle even the most placid visitors. It wasn't until months later that we would learn of a "secret room" in a back building where additional dogs were held in the dark. This building was more like a shed. Like The Warehouse, it had no natural light. To make matters worse, there was no electricity and the cage floors had rotted, leaving the dogs behind bars often yelping in pain as their paws fell through the rotted holes in the floor boards.

We began volunteering once a week and then twice. Every free moment we had outside of classes, studies and our training and competitions for the indoor track, outdoor track and cross-country team, we drove to the forgotten corner of town and spent hours upon hours with the imprisoned animals.

Todd left us to our own devices. He stayed in his small building off to the side from the others. We would always stop in and say good-bye as we left each time and he would be leaning back in his chair puffing away on that old cigarette. As ghastly as it may sound, more than a decade and a half later, Todd is still the most compassionate open intake shelter or pound director we have met to date. I wish it wasn't so, but Todd shines above the others we would meet as time marched on. Compassion, among other things, somehow is always missing in our nation's city shelter and county pound directors. Job requirements focused on obedience and adherence to the random stipulations of keeping the cages empty at all costs, rather than trying to help the animals that the facility "serves and protects".

By our second visit to the dilapidated shelter, we had opened every cat cage in the room, letting them run free. The cats had a window and each took turns looking out into the world, some perhaps for the first time in years. A few cats jumped on top of the long heavy lights hanging from the ceiling and knowing they were happy to move around, we laughed in delight. We made hundreds of toys so that every cage had several variations to help numb the sting of solitude when we placed them back in their cages. Each visit, we thoroughly cleaned every litter box and gave them fresh food and water. We lined their wire crates with newspaper so their paws found a soft place to land (we collected old newspapers and brought them with us). We were college students and didn't have much extra money, but when we had some to spare we would buy treats to give the cats on our visits. In time, we developed a system during every visit, we let ten cats out of their cages to play, rotating until everyone had a taste of freedom for the day. On rare occasion, Todd would walk over to the small building and crack the door open to ask if everything was going okay. He may have thought we were crazy, two twenty-year olds spending our free time playing with cats; but we didn't think a thing about it. We were exactly where we wanted to be.

After spending half of the day with the cats, we would move on to the dogs. For the first few months of volunteering, we would choose five dogs to walk at once. We would secure them into collars and leashes and take off into the city surrounded by fast-moving cars with tinted windows and booming music, often strolling through deserted parks. We would walk the group of dogs for a mile and head back for another batch. We walked Pit-Bulls and Rottweiler's, Chihuahua's and mixed breeds. At the time, we didn't know the labels given to any of the breeds; we only knew that they needed exercise and fresh air. We knew intuitively that they needed love.

Eventually we discovered a large fenced area in the back of the buildings. The grass was tall and the area had clearly never been used. *Another forgotten place.* Our young minds saw the unused space as an opportunity. That very day, without asking permission, we giggled like children as we took the dogs from their unsightly cages, one by one, and released them into the fenced back yard. After an hour we had every dog from the shelter out in the yard together. It never occurred to us that some dogs may not get along with others. It never crossed our minds that most of the dogs were unaltered. We only knew we wanted them to experience life, rather than to simply rot away in the forgotten building. If we could bring them one good day, we knew they would be happier for it. We didn't have any dog toys, but we found old branches and tossed them to the larger dogs. We kneeled on the ground to pet the small and senior canines and our eyes danced as we watched every one of them trot and run in the forgotten space, taking in the fresh air that touched their bodies, some for the first time in years. Todd wandered out into the yard after hearing our shouts of play and I turned just in time to see him shake his head, that darn cigarette hanging permanently from the corner of his mouth. Before I could blink, he had disappeared back into his office and we continued to play.

In all of our years at the shelter, we continued the tradition of letting the dogs run free together in the yard while we played with them and gave them attention (and we did the same for the cat room). Never once did we encounter an altercation between the dogs. They loved the sweet taste of freedom and it was clear that they weren't going to do anything to lose those moments of rare bliss.

During our last two years of undergraduate school, we scheduled a date once a year where the entire women's track team came to volunteer at the city animal shelter. Some spent time with cats and others helped walk the dogs throughout the city.

We continued volunteering several times a week as the years marched on and we grew closer to earning our degrees. We flew to Stanford, rode charter buses to Duke and everywhere in between for our competitive races (track and cross-country) and each time we returned, we found ourselves covered in pet fur in a forgotten corner of the city. One day as we entered the cat room, we noticed an elderly cat who stood motionless in her rusty cage, a malnourished kitten draped lifelessly over her boney back. The older cat had long brittle gray fur that fell off in clumps with each new breath. One eye held steady on us, the other was missing and left in its place was a socket full of fresh oozing blood and infection. We reached in to hold her and felt every bone in her frail body. The little beige kitten wasn't fairing any better. We carried them across the gravel yard and into Todd's office to ask about them. Where had they come from? What happened to the older cats eye? Could they get some veterinary care? By that point, we had been talking with veterinarians in the area to see if they would be willing to donate some of their time to the forgotten shelter. We were dismissed as "dumb kids" time and again, until one veterinarian said *maybe*. That maybe got us fired up. We pitched the idea to Todd and he said it wasn't possible. We tried time and again to bring veterinarians to the shelter. We offered to drive shelter pets to the veterinarian's office. We offered everything we could think of to provide the shelter pets at least minimal veterinary care, but our efforts were to no avail.

The frail, elderly one-eyed gray cat had been turned in a few days before, Todd explained. Their best guess was that someone had purposely gouged her eye out. The kitten who was with her wasn't hers; they just didn't have anywhere else to place him. And so the two numb souls sat huddled together in a bottom cage, waiting for...nothing. No veterinary care was coming. No one would adopt either sick cat. They were simply waiting to rot away like the building itself had been doing for years before our arrival.

"Could we adopt them?" I blurted out instinctively. Todd shrugged his shoulders nonchalantly.

"Sure, just need to see your driver's license. That old one, she won't make it another night." He took a long puff of his cigarette as he filled out a yellowed piece of paper. "You can have her for free. She'll never make it."

We clung to the two cats, knowing if we adopted them, we could take them in for desperately needed veterinary care. And a minute later, we found ourselves saving our first two shelter cats – embarking on what would soon evolve into Advocates 4 Animals, Inc.

We named the elderly gray cat Princess. After taking the frail cat to a veterinarian and spending

$500 on surgery for her gouged eye, my parents stopped talking to me. Clearly unhappy with how I choose to spend the minimal money I had as a college student, they shook their heads in disapproval. A month later we shelled out a few hundred dollars more for Princess as it was discovered her uterus was falling apart internally. We had her spayed and vaccinated and each day she grew stronger. Her hair grew in healthy and full, she threw her tail in the air as she trotted through the house and after more than a month of coaxing her to eat, she finally began eating on her own. Her emaciated 4-pound adult body grew into a healthy 12-pounds. Princess inspired our logo for Advocates 4 Animals and despite all that she had endured, despite the dire warning Todd had given us that Princess would not last one more night, she lived 10 more years.

Sadly, the kitten we saved with her passed away within a week. In his severely malnourished state, he had been given a strong dose of adult flea preventative at the shelter, which had ultimately killed him. Although no vetting was provided at the shelter, a company representative donated the flea medications as a promotion and shelter workers had not been versed on how to administer the medications (the adult version was too strong for his weak kitten body).

We saved a handful of others from that particular shelter prior to moving away from the city after college graduation, and we hung posters and flyers on every free light post and telephone pole encouraging others to adopt a rescue pet as well. Adoptions at the shelter saw an increase and we hoped this was a step forward. Sadly, the shelter never forged a relationship with a veterinarian. Todd left the shelter the year after we had graduated and moved out-of-state. A few years later we learned that the forgotten shelter was condemned. As for us, we continued leading a life covered in pet fur. After countless years spent volunteering in shelters, pounds, sanctuaries and working at various veterinary hospitals, kennels and operating a pet-sitting business, we pressed on to co-found an organization that existed to specifically help shelter pets. We set out to reform the shelter system. We were two girls on a mission of compassion, a mission of humane treatment for the millions of voiceless victims needlessly dying in shelters and pounds each year through no fault of their own. And today, that mentality hasn't changed. We're still two girls, albeit a bit older, on a mission to transform the grim reality of shelter pets into a reality of thriving existence. We're still fighting the same battles, one shelter and pound at a time. We're initiating viable programs to combat the tired mentality of shelter and pound directors who continue to embrace killing as a method of population control.

We've helped transform high-kill shelters into No Kill facilities, one at a time. In our own county, we've worked relentlessly for more than 11 years to work with our own county pound (which saves a mere 18% of healthy, friendly cats who enter their doors each year). After more than a decade of persistence, we're now the first approved rescue to be given permission to pull death row cats from this facility. But we still have a long way to go. After more than a decade of operating Advocates 4 Animals, we have established a handful of robust programs to combat our local pound's tired and outdated policies. Collaboration is generally the best route for helping the animals, but when you have a slaughter-house (aka high-kill county pound) that refuses to embrace *any* life-saving measures, you do your best to keep animals out of their "care" by any and all means. Over the years, in addition to our rescue/rehabilitation/adoption program, we have established a pet food pantry to provide temporary pet food assistance to families facing financial hardship. By providing pet food, families are able to keep their pets with them, rather than relinquish them to the pound and a terrible fate. We have established an affordable spay/neuter program for cats within our own county, again to help humanely control the pet population and to keep pets from being turned in to the pound. We have a Community Cats program which works to train and assist the public in TNR (trap-neuter-release) for feral cats. These, among other programs are helping us lower the rate of animals entering the local pound; therefore decreasing the number of needless deaths perpetuated by that very pound.

Across the country, additional animal rescue/ adoption, spay/neuter program and pet food pantry programs are urgently needed. One of the most popular questions asked is "How can I start a rescue?" It's not a simple one-word answer. If you do it right, you are actively helping animals in need. It may look "easy" to those on the outside, but as with anything worth doing, the endeavor of creating a non-profit (i.e. for purpose) animal welfare organization is filled with endless hard work, dedication, compassion, and perhaps most importantly a strong business sense. Yes, operating an animal rescue or animal welfare organization is a business. If you're considering starting an animal rescue organization, you must have a plan in place and you must operate as a business.

The chapters ahead outline the basics of what you'll need to consider prior to starting your own organization. While the need for helping animals is ever-present, the need for creating a viable, sustainable organization is essential. Don't fret: if you do not want to start your own organization and you're simply interested in understanding more about animal rescue this book is for you too! Whether you wish to help one or two animals a year through fostering for an organization, or you hope to start your own organization, this book is for you. The chapters ahead share the fundamental elements necessary to start an animal welfare organization *the right way*. In addition, we share our own experiences with you along the way. From hilarious mishaps to tough lessons, we share some of our most memorable stories throughout the book in hopes of helping you find your own path toward helping animals. Although everyone's journey will be unique, we can promise you one thing; if you devote even a portion of your life to helping animals in need, you will, at times be blissfully covered in pet fur.

SPECIAL NOTE: Many chapters in this book are followed by a "challenge" page which consists of both thought-provoking and action seeking questions to consider in regard to your own community and the animals you wish to help.

I

PAWS & CONSIDER THE FACTS...

_____

WHILE WAITING ON A FOSTER HOME SPACE to become available, we asked the Good Samaritans who contacted us at Advocates 4 Animals to help a mom cat and her newborn babies, if they could safely keep her inside of their home until we had an opening two days later. They agreed and we were happy to have space to help. We work to save death row shelter pets on a daily basis and we work to combat cats ever entering the shelter through our rescue/adoption program. All of our foster/adoptable pets are housed in individual volunteer foster homes and the number of lives we can save is always dependent on the number of quality, trained foster homes we have in our network. The constant pressure to help is enormous as it comes from pet guardians wanting to surrender their pets for one reason or another, from strays found in the public, from abuse and neglect cases, from feral cat colonies and from local kill shelters. Add to that, in 2013 our local pound only saved a mere 18% of "healthy, adoptable" cats and kittens. The pressure that we face on a day-to-day basis is life versus death. If we don't step up to help, there are no "back-up's" to call on in our area.

But I digress...two days later we were elated to help a mom cat and her newborn kittens and we traveled to the address given to rescue them. We knocked on the door to the house several times prior to receiving an answer. The door creaked open as a large dog lunged toward us. The man was confused and the home was dark. I waited outside by the car, ready with food and water. Amy walked into the house and let the door close behind her as the dog stayed close at her heels, watching her every move. The man retreated to an even darker basement and a moment later appeared with a sealed Tupperware container which he handed over. The mom and her newborn kittens were inside. Amy scurried out of the house as quickly as she could and as she approached the car, she threw open the lid to the box and we found that only one kitten remained alive. The box was full of steam as the mom cat had urinated and defecated while sealed in the box for two days. They all sat in the dampness of her excrement. The one newborn baby who had survived was barely hanging on. His eyes were not open yet and he was gasping for air; it had been too long. Meanwhile, the mom cat took in her first few breaths of fresh air in days. She was covered in the wetness of her own waste, terribly emaciated and dangerously dehydrated. We poured a fresh bowl of water and watched her lap up the smooth liquid with enthusiasm. Next, we opened a can of wet cat food and she devoured the food with vigor. Afterwards, she moved toward her only surviving kitten to bathe him and curled up in a ball amongst the nest of blankets provided in her large pet crate. The gray and white mom cat wasn't more than a year old herself. We named her Libby and sadly, her remaining baby did not survive the night. Exhausted and defeated, we knew Libby appreciated the constant love, affection, fresh food, water and veterinary care; but her heart was broken.

After nearly two months of physical and emotional rehabilitation in her foster home, we were working on a project to save three death row shelter kittens. Libby's foster mom agreed to foster the kittens, along with Libby. Magically within moments of being introduced to each other, Libby began to mother the three orphaned kittens (new fosters). She bathed them, cuddled with them and watched over them and as she did this, her own broken heart began to heal.

The need for the rescue of companion animals is astounding. United States shelters currently kill more than 50% of adoptable cats and dogs annually; a number that can be drastically reduced as additional qualified rescue organizations are established and as competent, compassionate shelter directors are hired. In our own county, less than 18% of healthy, adoptable cats left the pound alive in 2013; while a mere 30% of healthy, adoptable dogs left the shelter doors alive. The rest left in body bags, as if they never existed or mattered. Those innocent pets who are left in body bags were owner surrendered pets (guardians who said they were moving, didn't have enough time for the pet, had a baby, had sudden allergies, et cetera), they were feral cats who could have lived out their lives on one of the many local farms after being altered, they were neglected and abused pets who hid in the back of their cramped cages afraid someone new might harm them. They were senior pets who the shelter saw as "unadoptable" and unwanted. They were special needs pets who may have looked a bit different but could have lived long, happy, healthy lives nonetheless. They were black cats and dogs, who because of the color of their fur, are quickly deemed "unadoptable" as they are often not the first pick among adopters. They were living, breathing lives who wanted a chance to survive, but due to one shelter director's daily decisions, they didn't get that chance. Their fate decided for them by those who turned them into the shelter; the decision to kill them being finalized by the shelter director.

We've worked with countless open intake

shelters as they begin their journeys to become No Kill communities. It is possible to work together when a collaborative effort is established. In our own county, we worked for 11 years until we were finally given clearance as the first approved rescue organization to work with the pound to pull *some* of the death row pets. It's a start, but a great deal more is needed. While in the shelter recently to save a batch of orphaned kittens, a terrified young mom cat and her two-week old kittens sat in one of the nearby cages. Our volunteer asked if we could pull them too. She explained that she had room to foster a new feline family in need now. The director said the mom cat was "feral" (although she appeared to simply be scared in the cramped, loud environment of the shelter). Our foster volunteer said that she didn't mind if the mom cat was scared and she was willing to work with her on socialization. In addition, she offered that if the mom was feral, she lived on several acres of land and had heated cat huts and would allow the altered cat to live freely on her property once she weaned the babies. The shelter director shot her down instantly, fighting for what he saw as control and telling her "I'm not comfortable with that."

Instead of letting the cat live, instead of letting the cat go to a foster home and eventually a forever home, he saw the death of a nursing mom cat as a better solution. A week later, we received a call that the two orphaned kittens needed rescue and bottle feeding. Their mom was no longer here to do the feeding (the shelter had killed her). Although we have made great strides in being "approved" to pull from the local pound, the work is far from done.

Pets in need are all ages, breeds and sizes. One day while at the shelter to save several cats, we came across two large adult cats huddled together in their small cage. The cats were owner surrendered and no veterinary paperwork or records had been left, they hadn't even passed along their names. There they sat, huddled together, holding each other in their dark cage, not knowing what would happen next. We knew they were next in line to leave in a body bag that day. After making a few calls to our foster homes, we were able to secure a foster home for the two of them together in our network and we successfully pulled the two adult cats to safety. They had been previously spayed/neutered and declawed and on the ride home they continued to hold each other, the female wrapping her arms around the back of the male.

Rescue is needed when it's done the right way. Over more than a decade of working in animal rescue, we've encountered both rescues and shelters who operate on the fly. That's when things quickly go south for the animals. All too often, those who start a rescue organization have big hearts but a lack of business sense. They want to save the animals, their intentions are positive, but the follow through is lacking. When you agree to take in an animal as a foster pet in your rescue, the animals must receive proper testing and veterinary care prior to entering the foster homes (more on this later). It is also important to verify that the personal pets in the foster home are up to date on vaccinations, healthy and spayed/neutered. Furthermore, the new pet must be the right match for the new foster home. If you have a terribly shy or frightened pet and you place him in a lively foster home with children and other pets, issues are going to arise quickly. Operating an animal rescue isn't just about saving the animals. It's about providing proper veterinary care for every pet (first and foremost spay/neuter), proper food, water, shelter and adequate love, attention and rehabilitation training. In addition, how will you find qualified adopters for each of your pets? What will you do if you have an aggressive pet? Rescuing the pet is just the tip of the iceberg. What follows requires a strong business model, hard work and one of the most important aspects of running any business...great communication skills!

When individuals contact you for assistance, reply within 48 hours of their request and always offer guidance. Operating an animal rescue organization is a 24/7 business; you don't get a break on holidays or birthdays. Although taking in every pet that requires help is not possible, you can always offer other resources to provide a solution to help the animal. **Your words have the power to help, as much as your actions.**

When my dog passed away from old age, I was devastated. Her name was Grandma and we rescued her from a shelter after she was deemed vicious and unadoptable. She was a senior dog at the time and in horrible health. She was a foster pet turned forever pet for me. She fit in great with my other two rescue dogs and we had three wonderful years together before she passed. At Advocates 4 Animals, our rescue focus is on cats. After a bit of time, I felt ready to save another senior dog in need and I began my search. I contacted shelters, pounds and rescue organizations in search of a senior dog who needed help. I wanted to provide a senior dog with a loving home, who would otherwise not have one. But my search only lead to endless frustration and for the first time, I found myself on the opposite side of the adoption table. Instead of being the foster mom who helped potential adopters find the right match, I was now the potential adopter in search of assistance. Or rather, I should say I was in search of a reply! We contacted close to twenty area rescues, shelters and pounds and in the first week we only were able to actually speak with two. One was a kill shelter in Indiana who had four potential senior dogs needing help, but the individual we spoke with didn't know anything about them. The other was a dog focused rescue organization who was pleasantly responsive and helpful. As for the other 18 organizations, we were left without a reply. We called, left countless messages, wrote emails introducing ourselves and even filled out adoption applications...all were left without a reply. More than a month after the inquiries, (and after we had found and adopted a special needs senior dog from the local dog rescue organization who had kindly responded the same week we contacted them) we received two more replies that were short and unhelpful. One said they wanted to know which dog we were interested in (even though it clearly stated the dog's name in our original email they were replying to) the other reply said that they would work on getting back to us. We never heard back from any of the others. It was a real wake-up call for what adopters were experiencing! It wasn't just from pounds or shelters, it was from rescue organizations too. The lack of response was disheartening. Our focus from the beginning at Advocates 4 Animals has always been responsiveness and communication (and it is difficult when hundreds of emails, texts, and phone calls bombard you on a daily basis) but it is do-able if you make communication one of your priorities. It is a must for any successful business model. Without communication, you cannot find foster homes, adopters, donors, et cetera for your operation. Friendly, respectful and responsive communication is essential. Set specific hours during the work week and weekends which you will devote to e-mails, phone calls and other forms of communication and stick to it. As with any viable business, you will ride the roller-coaster of ups and downs. Be sure to realize that your top concerns are the welfare of the animals in your care and your daily communications with potential adopters, your foster homes, volunteers and potential donors.

At Advocates 4 Animals, it's always our goal to provide each potential adopter with a positive experience so in the future, if they decide to add to their furry family, they will choose to adopt a rescue pet again. Whether it's from us or another rescue or shelter organization, our goal is to promote the adoption of rescue pets and to help each adopter have a memorable experience that they will then share with others. With over eight million rescue pets waiting for homes annually in our country alone, we need to do everything we can to promote adoption into loving, committed homes.

CHAPTER 1 CHALLENGE:

- What are the euthanasia statistics at your local pound and/or shelter? What are their intake numbers and where are the majority of their intakes coming from (i.e. owner surrenders, senior pets, ill pets, etc.?) Is the shelter/pound an open-intake facility? Is their director willing to work with local 501(c)3 rescue organizations?

- How many 501(c)3 rescue organizations are in your area? Are they volunteer-based? Do they have facilities? What is each rescue organizations main focus (i.e. dogs under 10-pounds, a specific breed of dog, et cetera)?

- How many 501(c)3 organizations work to help feral cats in your area (through TNR methods)?

2

WHAT'S THE DIFFERENCE?

———————

IT COMES DOWN TO EFFORT, commitment and creativity. Thinking outside of the proverbial box is essential if you want to champion the No Kill movement. Too often, shelters and pounds stuck in the stone age of traditional kill methods, argue that killing is the only way to combat the myth of pet overpopulation. My response...how's that working for you? More importantly, how is that working for the animals? The answer is, quite simply, *it's not*. Statistics tell the story. DoSomething.org shares that homeless animals outnumber homeless people 5 to 1. Shelters kill approximately 4 million cats and dogs every year in United States shelters.

And yes, you can re-read the statement above. I said the *myth* of pet overpopulation. Not only can we reduce shelter pet euthanasia, we can eliminate needless shelter killing. This fact is proven in communities throughout the country such as those in California, Virginia, Utah, Kansas, Nevada and more. In a Local Channel 13 Florida News interview Nathan Winograd, founder of the No Kill Advocacy Center, discusses the fact that some of the most successful No Kill Communities have been established in both urban and rural areas. Some No Kill Communities have been established where communities are highly conservative. Others have been created where communities are predominantly liberal. As Winograd stated, it just goes to show you "...when it comes to saving the lives of dogs and cats, people of all walks of life want to build a better world for them."

Winograd has created what he calls the No Kill Equation. The equation is proving successful in a growing number of communities. The mandatory programs and services that shelters/pounds must implement in order to become No Kill communities include:

- TNR Program (Trap/Neuter/Release)
- High-volume, low-cost spay/neuter options
- Rescue groups
- Foster care
- Comprehensive adoption programs
- Pet retention
- Medical Rehabilitation
- Behavioral Rehabilitation
- Public relations/community involvement
- Volunteers
- Proactive Redemptions
- A compassionate shelter director

In order to create a true No Kill environment, communities must implement every element of the No Kill Equation successfully. Take a look at the items on the above list. Does your shelter implement any of these programs/services? How can you work with them to help implement the programs/services that are not yet being utilized by your local pound/shelter? Do you know others interested in volunteering? Have you considered fostering a shelter pet? Do you know individuals interested in helping with a TNR program?

Many naysayers of the No Kill movement continue to tout that No Kill communities are unattainable and unrealistic. They say there are not enough taxpayer dollars to fund a No Kill effort. Interestingly enough, using taxpayer dollars to save the lives of shelter pets is more cost-effective than the unnecessary, daily killing that takes place behind the closed doors of shelters throughout this country. Killing animals costs more than adopting them. Adoptions bring in funds to the shelter. In addition, when shelters partner with local 501c3 non-profit rescue organizations, animals not only get to live, but the cost of care for the animals is then transferred from using taxpayer dollars to private donations. This is a winning situation for everyone: the animals, the community/taxpayers and for the adopters, of course!

Embracing the No Kill Equation saves lives and saves tax-payer dollars. Tax dollars in our local county pay for the killing of 82% of "healthy adoptable cats", 100% of feral, shy and scared cats and 100% of ill, injured, senior or special needs pets. Furthermore, these same tax-payers are shelling out their funds to kill more than 70% of "healthy adoptable" dogs and 100% of scared, shy, special needs, senior, abused/neglected or potentially aggressive dogs. If the pound hired a compassionate, competent director, one who believed in utilizing the No Kill model, those numbers could be drastically reduced. Instead of spending tax-dollar money each year to kill, they could be saving 90% or more of the lives in need who enter their doors and *earning money* instead of spending. How? Charge approved 501(c)3 rescue organizations a set fee to pull each pet to safety (i.e. $5 pull fee for an approved local organization to pull an un-vetted pet). Instead of spending money to temporarily house the pet, feed the pet and then needlessly kill the pet, the shelter would spend $0 and bring in $5 while also saving a life. It's a transparent system that works.

We've worked with dozens of open intake shelters to assist them in the transformation from a kill mentality to embracing No Kill measures. Every shelter presents a new challenge, as it's a new set of faces, a new director and a stubborn and tired mentality that killing is the *only* way. But, the only way to what? What are we trying to achieve? As animal shelters, pounds and rescue agencies, aren't we all working to help the animals? One would hope, but all too often that's not the case. In shelters and pounds with paid employees, for many, it's nothing more than a job; a pay-check. So how do you change the mentality of people who are apathetic about the lives of animals in the first place? It all starts with the director and you. As a professional rescue organization (or as an individual who wishes to see change for the better) you have the power to begin creating positive change in your own local shelter. Even when it seems impossible, you can create a change. Be ready to hang on for the ride and never let go of your persistence. As mentioned previously, it has taken us 11 years to make headway with our own county pound. We're now the first approved rescue organization to be able to pull death row cats from the pound, but it's a work in progress and we still have a long way to go. Sadly, this is often not an overnight battle, but with tenacity and persistence, we can transform one shelter at a time, one city at a time, and one state at a time.

Motivated shelters and those who embrace the No Kill equation set up a multitude of methods to reach approved 501(c)3 rescue organizations, potential adopters, foster homes and donors. These same shelters hold adoption event days, are active on social media and have a strong online website presence. Often, these same shelters develop a trusted network of volunteers who help with transporting pets to and from veterinary visits, to and from adoption events, and to local approved rescue organizations who are able and willing to pull pets from that particular shelter (to create more space for the shelter).

As a 501(c)3 rescue organization, you can begin working with your local shelter/pound in a variety of ways. It's important to present yourself in a professional, well-organized manner when approaching city council or your county pound director. Once you have pulled the necessary statistics and have created a plan of action to actively help reduce the number of deaths in that particular pound/shelter, the next step is to create a friendly, comprehensive proposal and deliver it to the shelter director. Once the proposal is delivered, schedule an in-person meeting with the director to discuss your proposal face to face. This is not always the most comfortable meeting. Often the director will worry that you are trying to "take control" of their facility. It's important to let them know loud and clear that your intention is to work WITH them to assist them in saving lives. Believe me, this conversation is often difficult. As we chipped away year after year at our own county pound, it tore us apart as we received the annual statistics, knowing that we could have reduced the killing had they accepted our help. As they ignored our requests to help again and again, we used that as fuel to create innovative programs for our local community to keep pets out of the shelter altogether. It worked. The intake numbers at the county pound have reduced each year since the implementation of our programs (even prior to being able to pull death row pets directly from the shelter). After eleven years of persistence, embarking on the beginnings of a relationship to save pets who would otherwise needlessly be killed in the shelter is exciting as we move forward. Now, we not only have a handful of viable programs to combat the chance of pets ending up in the shelter, but we have access to pull death row cats when space is available in our foster homes. It is a start.

We've heard tales of other rescue organizations who march into a pound or shelter and declare they are going to take over or they are going to fight the shelter until they embrace No Kill methods. This, in our opinion, is not the way to long-term success. And clearly, this did not bring the groups the results they wanted. In most cases, the shelter directors banned the rescue groups from ever entering the facility. No one wants to feel threatened. If you were eating your favorite flavor of ice cream and enjoying each bite (let's say your favorite flavor is orange sherbet) and someone marches up to you and demands that you drop your ice cream and eat chocolate ice cream instead because it's much more delicious, you're instantly going to cling to your prized orange sherbet and ignore the lunatic making demands. Anyone who feels threatened will instantly go into survival mode. And you don't want to blow your chance at building a positive relationship with your local shelter/pound. Now imagine you're eating your favorite ice cream and someone smiles kindly at you and casually strolls up and asks if you would be interested in having a few "free orange sherbet" ice cream coupons that they happen to have. Of course you would eagerly agree because you're getting something you want; your favorite ice cream – for free! Why would you argue? *It's all in the approach.*

All too often, shelter directors who are killing animals day after day have grown numb to the concept of death. They don't view what they're doing as wrong; justifying the killing as a "part of the job". But your job, as an impactful rescue organization, is to kindly approach the shelter director and let them know how you can ease their burden. Let them know how you can help them. It's not about the politics of saying one organization is better than the other, it's about finding a way to successfully forge a collaboration that works in favor of the animals. A collaboration that actively saves lives. Don't make this a power struggle and don't make it personal. It's about the voiceless victims, the innocent animals who are waiting behind bars, wishing a local rescue existed; hoping for your professionalism and persistence to pay off so you can save them before their time is up. They are waiting as you read this. They are waiting as you design your plan and they are hoping you'll create your organization the right way so you can spare their life, because most likely, you are their only hope of ever leaving the shelter alive.

Remember, it's about what *your organization* can offer the shelter. How can you help them empty their cages? How can you increase their bottom line? How can you help save tax-payer dollars? Create a solid plan and then get ready for action. Make it clear that you don't want to take any of their highly adoptable pets that they, themselves, can properly adopt. You want to help where help is needed. If they have trouble placing senior pets, maybe that's where you come in. If their biggest need is with orphaned kittens (who need around the clock care and bottle-feeding) and you have retired volunteers who are willing to provide this care, let them know that is your specialty and you can help there. Whatever your niche, let it be known and work really hard to keep getting better at what you do.

What is an Open Intake shelter versus a Limited Intake shelter?

You may have heard the terms before, but do you understand the implications of each concept? An open intake shelter must accept any and all companion animals regardless of health, temperament, or space available, with no limitation. Often this type of shelter or pound will have "drop-boxes" located in the front of their facility allowing pet guardians to simply drop-off their pet in an overnight area (generally this consists of a small area filled with crates outside of the facility). Open intake shelters cannot turn an animal away even if they are full or if the animal is sick or severely injured.

A limited intake shelter may accept companion animals on a voluntary and/or space available basis. Admissions may be subject to health and/or temperament criteria, or any other criteria that the shelter may designate based on its mission.

When it comes to open intake versus limited intake shelters one is not better or worse than the other, they simply have different rules.

Both types of shelters can successfully be No Kill facilities. For limited intake shelters, the No Kill mission can be easier because their intake is...well, *limited* based on what they can financially afford and physically hold. Open intake shelters may need additional creativity and persistence to achieve No Kill status, but this goal is achievable and sustainable with the right director as the shelter leader. This encouraging fact has been proven again and again such as with the Grayson County SPCA in Kentucky and the Nevada Humane Society. The Nevada Humane Society, for example, was an extremely high kill shelter prior to gaining new leadership – *compassionate leadership.* Reno Nevada's humane society changed everything and their Executive Director Bonney Brown is now the winner of two awards from the national No Kill Advocacy Center. Change is possible.

Rescue organizations are often operated out of residential spaces – at least in their initial stages. Many rescues operate using a volunteer foster home model, like Advocates 4 Animals (working with dozens of volunteer foster homes in the area). Rescues are generally limited intake organizations, only being able to take in what they have space to accommodate at the time. Keep in mind, there are dangers for rescues that operate with only *one* home acting as the facility and sole foster home for the organization. If one home / person accumulates too many animals, the illness and stress rates will be a factor in the well-being of the pets you have rescued. It is extremely important to set limits, whether you are a one-home operation or a large, volunteer foster home based organization. Setting limits for your own home, as well as setting a limit for each foster home within your organization, is essential for long-term success and for the care of the animals. [More on setting adequate limits in a later chapter.]

CHAPTER 2 CHALLENGE:

- Now that you've collected data on your local pounds/shelters and existing rescue organizations, identify which are open intake and which are limited intake agencies. Next, identify which are kill shelters and which organizations embrace the No Kill equation.

- How can you help your local shelter/pound? Can you reasonably pull 1 cat/dog per week? 10 a month? Can you help create active social media pages? Can you help establish a foster program? Can you help create and facilitate adoption events and open-house events for the shelter? Can you find professional photographers to donate their time to come to the shelter to take photographs of the adoptable pets for a stronger online presence? Do you have approved foster homes in place for senior pets and can you help pull this type of pet from the shelter (ones they have deemed "unadoptable")?

3

THE KEY TO CREDIBILITY IS SPECIFICITY

———

I rescue cats.

Okay, let's get more specific.

I prefer to help special needs cats.

Dig a bit deeper.

I enjoy helping blind cats.

Who do you want to rescue: stray cats/shelter cats?

Okay. Let's put it all together in one statement.

Our organization works to save the lives of blind shelter cats in need of rescue.

You've just created the beginnings of your mission statement.

It is imperative to make your mission statement specific. Who will you help? Where will you help? Where will the pets be housed while they are waiting for adoption? What vetting will you provide upon their intake? Will you only work with a specific age, breed or weight of pet?

You can choose to rescue cats, dogs, birds, bunnies, horses, goats, chickens...believe me, unfortunately there is a need for any avenue you choose. Once you decide on the type of animal you are going to rescue, take some time to think about the particulars. Will you rescue orphaned animals only? Will you rescue only senior animals? Special needs pets? Think about where you will place each animal and the type of care they will require prior to making this decision.

Side Note: *We highly recommend that you rescue one pet of your intended specification as you start. Foster this pet in your home and learn about him/her. What type of special care do they need? Can you handle multiple types of this pet at once? How will you train your volunteers (or volunteer foster families) to handle this type of pet? How will you handle the veterinary expenses for the pets you are saving?*

Consider the following facts as you decide what the focus of your organization will be.

Did you know?

- Dark colored pets are most often last chosen for adoption in shelters (and most often euthanized first)?

- Cats are the number one breed/pets killed in United States shelters (*Followed by Chihuahua's and then Pit-Bulls*).

- Special needs pets are often not placed up for

adoption in U.S. shelters due to what some directors view as "lack of adoptability".

- Senior pets are often over-looked in shelters.

- *Most* county pounds and shelters kill 100% of feral, shy and scared cats.

- Owner relinquished dogs (at pounds and shelters across the country) are most often between 8 months young and 2 years old — the age where positive reinforcement training is most needed (i.e. potty training, chewing, high-activity level, et cetera).

What will your focus be? Where does the greatest need for the animals meet your interest and ability level?

Honing down your mission statement is key to your organization's future success. Without a proper mission statement (i.e. very specific focus), the task at hand becomes quickly overwhelming and can result in compassion fatigue. When someone asks you what your organization *does*, your mission statement needs to clearly and concisely explain the answer.

In addition to your mission statement, be clear on what area you are serving. Will you serve one city, one county or a specific zip code? Set your boundaries before you get to work. Not doing so will result in an overwhelming amount of pleas for urgent assistance, which will have you running ragged all over the state – or the country – if you're not specific from the *get go*.

When we first began Advocates 4 Animals, we worked with shelters across the states of Kentucky, Ohio and Indiana. While we value that experience *(and at the time there were very few shelters willing to work with rescues – as rescues were fairly new to the scene)*, today we realize that by working with one or two counties and focusing all of our efforts in this specific area, we can make a larger impact.

For the first several years of operating Advocates 4 Animals, we said yes to virtually everyone who requested our help and we quickly became overwhelmed. At the time, we thought saying yes meant that we could make the biggest difference. The more lives you rescue, the more you help, right? Experience has taught us there is a delicate balance and the importance of a specific mission statement. It is crucial to know your limits and your volunteers (i.e. foster homes) limits as well. Some foster homes will say yes, I will help another one, when they hear the dire stories of the pets in need. As the director of the organization, you need to protect your volunteers as you do the pets in your care. If you overwhelm volunteers with too many pets, they will become exhausted and you will risk losing them as a foster parent for future pets within your organization. Talk to each foster parent prior to their start and set a limit. Are they willing to foster a mom and litter of kittens? Maybe their limit is 3 adult pets. Discuss what they are able and willing to handle and figure out how that fits into your program.

When we said yes to everyone requesting help, we lost any sense of normalcy in our life. Hard work and dedication are absolutely important, but setting boundaries is essential to good business practices and to quality care. Some pets that you foster will be more challenging than others. There are pets who won't get along with other pets, pets with multiple daily medications and special routines, pets who require a high amount of exercise, pets who require extensive training and assistance and there are pets who require constant medical care which can quickly result into mounting veterinary bills. It's important to remember that your foster parents may "quit" at any time. If they call you and say they have a family emergency and need to return their foster pet that evening, where will the pet go? Will they remain safe? Do you have a back-up plan? When you operate a rescue organization, you are not only caring for countless furry lives that are depending on your professionalism and dedication, but you have the lives of your volunteers to consider as well. It's a lot to juggle on any given day.

When we drove outside of our local area in response to a call for help, it was discovered cats filled the home – both dead and alive. Felines of all ages and sizes ran in and out of the open front door. Feces filled the kitchen sinks. No food or water bowls were found. None of the cats were altered and the stench of cat spray filled the walls, as did piles of cardboard boxes that reached the ceiling. Our volunteer was severely attacked by one of the cats as she walked through the home, leaving her in tears and with a nasty injury on her thigh. At the time, we weren't specific to the area where we would rescue. To make a long story short, our volunteer survived and we rescued every living cat, spayed/neutered each cat, emotionally rehabilitated and eventually placed each cat into a loving forever home through our adoption program. This rescue mission, among countless others, taught us a valuable lesson as we continued moving forward: we can't say yes to everyone. We can provide resources and suggestions, but *we* can't be the ones going out to rescue *every* pet in need in the entire state. We were just a small group of individuals wanting to make a difference. If we utilized our efforts closer to home and if we provided other avenues of assistance to those in need outside of our area, we realized we could make an even larger impact on lives in need.

In the early years of our organization, we found ourselves driving down the road in an unfamiliar area after returning multiple cats to their homes following spay and neuter surgeries with our veterinarian. Police lights filled the evening sky and we waited at a long stop light in the middle of town. When the light turned green, our heads turned to the left and our breath caught in unison at the sight of a neglected house on the hill. The boarded up house had only one remaining window. The lone window was spray painted to read:

FREE KITTENS INSIDE

While Amy walked up to the boarded up home, I had 9-1-1 dialed on my cell phone ready to push CALL at any sign of danger. Looking back, we know we put ourselves in harm's way; it wasn't our smartest idea. But we saved the only remaining kitten in the dark home where mattresses lined the floor. Rap music blared from every corner of the house and people rolled around on the floor in a haze everywhere you looked. We named the terrified tortoiseshell kitten Layla. As Amy ran from the house, I rolled down the window as she handed the trembling kitten into my hands. I dropped my cell phone to the floor, taking the frightened kitten into my hands and promising her that she would never feel fearful again. We were in our twenties and not much fazed us then; but looking back, we know we could have been smarter about the rescue itself. We try to learn something from every experience. Isn't that the best way to live our lives? We will never regret saving Layla.

I still remember her adoption day and sharing the story of her rescue with her adopter. Knowing that Layla was fully vetted, and now safe and loved forever was and is incredibly rewarding. I shudder to think about what her life may have become had we not stopped that day to enter the boarded up home.

Honing down your mission statement, as we discussed previously, is essential to long term success. When we were in the early years of Advocates 4 Animals, we rescued both cats and dogs. We rescued all sizes, ages, breeds, temperaments, backgrounds...you asked, we said yes. We thought that's how we could help. In those days, there weren't many rescue organizations in existence; there were no models to follow and we hadn't yet heard of Google or YouTube. We just knew we wanted to help. After a while, we experimented with different specifications to see what worked for us and for our growing set of volunteer foster homes. While we aim to share our experiences with you throughout this book, we know that stumbling is part of the process. You will forge your own path as you march ahead. You will learn your own set of lessons through trial and error; but our hope is that by sharing our stories and experiences with you, you can avoid some major pitfalls when you're first starting your organization (or when you are first beginning to help animals in need).

As the years marched on, we placed our focus on feline rescue for our adoption program. We still rescued and fostered the occasional dog, but our primary focus was (and is) on cats. Cats are the number one breed/pet killed in U.S. shelters; shelter death kills more cats than any disease. In addition, there were no existing resources for cats in need in our own county or anywhere near our area. In the early 2000's when we received a call regarding a hoarding case, we knew that it wasn't possible for us to take in all 40+ cats and dogs. The owners of the home felt they were doing the best they could for the pets in their care. They lived in the country and said that animals were dumped on their property repeatedly. They explained to us they never had money to spay and neuter the cats and dogs who came their way, but they always provided shelter, food and water for them. With none of the pets being altered, their numbers grew rapidly year after year. As the couple faced foreclosure, they panicked for the well-being of their animals. We inquired about the animals conditions and they conveyed to us that eight of the cats were blind or had another special need and those same eight were emaciated and in need of immediate veterinary care. The remaining thirty-some cats and dogs were generally healthy. After taking a few days to speak with our volunteer foster homes and to discuss it between ourselves, we agreed to take in the eight blind/special needs/emaciated (worst off) cats. Next, we supplied the direct contact information for multiple rescue organizations to help with the remaining pets. We asked the couple to take a photo of each remaining pet and send 2 or 3 photos of each pet to each rescue that we provided and ask them to help by taking in one, two or three pets. If every rescue could take in a few, all could find safety before the house foreclosed. With a lot of nudging and persistence, the plan worked.

All 40+ cats and dogs found proper rescue, were spayed/neutered and eventually placed into loving homes. As for the eight blind/special needs cats that we took into Advocates 4 Animals for this project, all were fully rehabilitated and adopted into forever homes with the exception of one. A petite black cat we named Helen (blind in both eyes due to severe eye infections that had been left untreated for years) lived with us for nearly one year before she passed away. Despite her difficult past, we provided Helen with unlimited love and affection during her time with Advocates 4 Animals. We did not seek adoption for her. While working closely with our veterinarian, we realized that she had ongoing health challenges that required consistent (and expensive) medical care. Helen learned to navigate her way around the house, played with toys that made noise (so she could track them) and snuggled up close. We knew going into this project that it was possible all eight cats would be in such need that they may need to stay with our organization for the duration of their lifetimes, no matter how long or short that may have been. It was an important aspect to note in this rescue, as you never know for sure when a pet will need long-term care. Being prepared is the name of the game. Just as with your own personal life journey, you never know exactly what a new rescue project will entail. Being prepared for expensive medical bills, aggressive behavior, severe trauma that requires extensive emotional rehabilitation of the pet or other abnormal circumstances can eliminate unnecessary stress as you move your organization forward.

CHAPTER 3 CHALLENGE:

- Draft your organization's mission statement.

- Map out a plan for veterinary care. Which veterinarian will you work with? Will they provide discounted services to you once you are an approved 501c3 organization? How much will a spay surgery cost for the type/weight of pet you will be rescuing? How much for a neuter? What are the costs of vaccinations? Flea preventative? De-wormers?

- Will your organization save stray pets? Owner relinquished pets? Or shelter pets? If you choose to work with shelter pets, does the shelter already work with existing rescue organizations? What criteria do they require to work together?

Remember that you can always add additional programs to support your mission statement down the road. Right now, as you're forming your organization, it is imperative to choose a specific mission (i.e. focus) and test it out on a small-scale.

TIP: Starting small is essential to the long-term success of your organization and for the animals in your care.

4

WHAT MAKES THEM STAY?

VOLUNTEERS ARE AT THE HEART OF ALL FOR PURPOSE (i.e. non-profit) organizations. When operating a rescue organization, at a minimum you will need qualified volunteers for your foster homes, to help as transport drivers, to help with fundraiser events and more. How do you plan on finding qualified volunteers to assist with your organization's mission? How will you screen them? Will you have an online application and then schedule a face-to-face (possibly in their home) meeting? Will you perform background checks prior to meeting potential foster homes? Will you check references? Will you make sure the potential foster homes resident pets are already spayed/neutered, vaccinated and good with other pets?

Once you have established a screening process for new volunteers, what is the next step that you can take that will allow you to know you can trust your volunteers to represent the organization in a positive light and to properly care for their assigned pet(s)?

Do you have a hotline established for your volunteer foster homes, where they can access you 24/7 in case of emergency? We recommend having a hotline as this can be essential to a pet's well-being. Although the rescued pets are placed in qualified foster homes, you must always remember that ultimately they are in your care as the director of the organization. Keeping that in mind, when you meet with your new volunteer foster homes, be sure to set an upfront pet limit that both of you are comfortable with. Be sure it is a limit that is reasonable for the foster parent(s). It is recommended that every new foster home start out with one adult pet to ensure they can handle the day-to-day duties required during fostering (before adding additional foster pets to the home).

Speaking of hotlines, when a pet in your organization needs emergency veterinary care (or any veterinary care), who will take them to the veterinarian? Will all foster homes be authorized to take their pets directly to your approved veterinarian(s)? Does your veterinarian have the name of all approved individuals?

At Advocates 4 Animals, we are fortunate to have grown a large volunteer foster home base. Our organization only authorizes our director and our CFO to take any foster pets in our care and to and from veterinary visits. On multiple occasions as we've continued to grow, we've had members of the public walk into our veterinarian's office and tell the staff that "we" authorized *them* to come to the veterinarian at *our* expense. In short, they try to tell the staff that they are bringing their cat in (it has been for expensive care in every case) and just to add it to the Advocates 4 Animals bill. We've worked with our veterinarians' office for nearly a decade and they know this is not how we operate. Again, we cannot stress the importance of communication and trust (with your veterinarians, volunteers, et cetera). Knowing our system, the veterinary staff called us in each instance to ask for our approval. However, had we not had a strong system established with our veterinarians, thousands of dollars would have been unknowingly added to our bill on several occasions.

As you search and screen potential volunteer foster homes, what process will you utilize to locate long-term committed foster homes (as opposed to fosters who prefer to do "2-weeks and done")? It is hard for pets to be bounced from one location to another, week after week. Finding qualified, committed foster parents is essential to the well-being of the pets in your organizations care.

Some of our foster parents at Advocates 4 Animals have been with us for more than a decade, while others prefer to foster a litter of kittens once a year – or possibly just once. Every foster home is different. Foster homes will have a wide variety of personalities, preferences, abilities, talents, environments/energies, et cetera. Keep in mind that you will need to properly match appropriate pets with appropriate foster parents/families in your program to ensure a good experience for everyone involved.

How will you train your new volunteers? Will you do the training? What will be included in the training? Will it be one-on-one as new foster homes are added, or will you host group sessions once a month?

Where will your headquarters be located? When foster homes need to bring their foster pet to you for one reason or another, where will they be bringing the pet (and picking them up)? Does the environment offer an open, friendly atmosphere?

How will you retain your quality volunteers? What forms of appreciation will you provide throughout the year? Appreciation does not have to be shown in the form of t-shirts or other gifts, demonstrate appreciation with a simple, genuine thank you. You can send a hand-written card of thanks or you can write a blog or post a thank you on your website and/or social media pages as well. Letting your volunteers know they matter and they are making a difference is essential to retention. They are volunteering with your organization because they believe in the cause; let them know their efforts are making a difference and tell them exactly how.

As the director of the organization, it is imperative that you demonstrate steady, calm, reliable and enthusiastic leadership on a day-to-day basis. Consistent communication, dedication and loyalty to the organization's cause are the keys to retaining volunteers and to moving your organization forward in a myriad of ways.

We have retired volunteers at Advocates 4 Animals who specialize in bottle-feeding orphaned kittens. We have volunteer foster homes that prefer only to foster senior pets. We have some that only want to foster a special needs pet. And we have others that will foster any new intake that we have a need for (once they are fully vetted of course) when they have an open spot in their home for fostering (i.e. once their current foster pet(s) has been successfully adopted).

What specializations do you hope to find with your own volunteer foster homes? Make a list of your dream team of foster homes. How many foster homes do you hope to have? In what location/zip code(s)? Knowing what you want (and need) is essential as you move ahead.

We've heard horror stories of fosters gone wrong in other organizations. We've heard of a foster cat climbing in the dryer. A guest in the home did not know to look for the cat and turned the dryer on. The cat did not survive. Cats and dogs darting out the front door (if the door is left ajar) and becoming lost – or worse, hit by a car. New foster homes being given orphaned pets to bottle-feed with no training or experience— in many cases the orphaned pet will not make it. For orphaned kittens, they need to be monitored (and fed) every 2-3 hours during their first several weeks of life; it is essential that your volunteers be properly trained and willing to wake up throughout the night (night after night) to provide proper care. The stories send chills down our spines. You work hard to save their lives. You don't want a hardship to occur to the animal while being fostered. Proper screening, followed by adequate training are vital to the well-being of the pets in your care and to the success of your organization.

CHAPTER 4 CHALLENGE:

- Do you have a committed group of volunteers as you start your organization? Are they willing to provide long-term foster care (possibly up to a year for some pets)?

- How will you train your volunteers as you begin your organization? Set a limit to have each foster home foster one pet and see how it goes as you begin.

- Do you have an established hotline for foster parents to reach you 24/7 in case of emergency?

- Who is approved to take pets from your organization into your veterinarian?

- If one of your foster parents goes on vacation

who will care for their foster pet(s) while they are away?

- Where will a pet go if you have a foster home suddenly quit?

- If you become ill or severely injured, who will operate the organization?

- How will you screen new potential foster homes for your organization?

- How will you show regular appreciation to your organization's volunteers? What unique ideas can you think of now that may help retain volunteers within your organization?

5

MAKING THE CONNECTION

_____

WE WORKED WITH DOZENS OF VETERINARIANS and clinics before we settled on one. Finding the right veterinarian(s) for your organization can be an especially difficult challenge without a solid plan in place. We recommend making a list of qualities you hope to find in your future veterinarian. Some examples are located below:

Has the veterinarian worked with other 501(c)3 organizations in the past (or currently)? Obtain a list of those organizations and contact each one to ask about their relationship. How long have they worked with this particular veterinarian? What are the pro's and con's for their organization?

Does the veterinarian provide the same quality services for pets within a rescue organization as they do for pets owned by the general public?

Does the veterinarian offer a discount on spay/neuter services for your 501(c)3 organization? What will the cost of surgeries be? What if the pet is in heat? What if the pet is pregnant? What if the pet is found to have pyometra? What are the costs of other services such as vaccines, testing and dental surgeries?

If you bring additional clients (i.e. your adopters) to their clinic via referrals, will the veterinarian's office offer you an additional discount on services rendered?

Will you hire your veterinarian to work in your organization's office/headquarters or will you simply bring pets to the veterinarian's office? If your veterinarian will be working exclusively for you, how will you ensure that you have enough funds to pay their salary? What will their salary be? How will you fund equipment purchases?

If you work with a local veterinarians office (you bring your pets to and from *their* office) if you have an emergency, will they work with you to squeeze you in that day? If you are working with feral cats, for example, will they allow you to bring the trapped cats in for spay/neuter within a day's notice?

How young will the veterinarian spay/neuter pets? What are the weight/age requirements? (i.e. kittens are spayed/neutered at 2 lbs. with many veterinarians)

You will discover additional questions to add as you begin thinking about the qualities you hope to find in your organization's veterinarian(s). It is also important to consider your veterinarian's demeanor and personality. Do you like working with them? Do you feel comfortable trusting the rescued pets with this particular veterinarian? What works for one organization (or individual) may not bode well for another. Do your research, schedule meetings with potential veterinarians; share your plan and ask questions.

Too often we have witnessed rescue

organizations choosing to work with clinics or veterinarians solely based on their fees. Understandably, they are trying to get the cheapest price; with the thought process being the cheaper they can get the surgeries/veterinary care, the more pets they can provide surgery for. But wait, not so fast! While cost is definitely a factor for 501(c)3 non-profit organizations, do not overlook quality care. Let me repeat, do not overlook quality care! This is not to say that veterinarian's offices (or hiring your own veterinarian) are better than high-volume/low-cost clinics. There are many high-volume clinics, open to the public and rescue organizations (with no income requirements) that offer high quality services. UCAN (United Coalition for Animals Non-Profit Spay/Neuter Clinic) in Cincinnati, Ohio is one such organization that provides top of the line care. Often you must book your appointments several months in advance (which requires accurate planning on your part) but the quality of service combined with the price is second-to-none. UCAN performs minimally invasive surgeries, they tattoo each cat's stomach so that it is always clear that the pet has been spayed/neutered (a future veterinarian would merely need to shave the cats stomach to view the tattoo for verification of the spay/neuter surgery) and they offer pain medication to pets following surgery. In addition, they operate in a clean and friendly environment. The clinic also offers microchips, vaccinations and disease testing. But beware, not all clinics operate in such a professional manner. Other clinics offer discounted services for spay/neuter to the public (and often times to rescue organizations as well) but they are skimping on the services rendered. For example, too often the pets are not given pain medications following surgery, they are not tattooed and unfortunately too many clinics do not operate in a clean facility. The same is true for veterinarians. Be sure to do your homework prior to working with any clinic or veterinarian. While cost effectiveness is important, attitudes, cleanliness and quality are essential to the well-being of pets in your organization's care.

Speaking of veterinary care, what basic services will you provide to each of the pets in your rescue organization? We recommend providing the following minimum services prior to a pet entering one of your organizations qualified foster homes:

- General Health Check

- Nail Trim

- Cats: FIV/FeLv combo test

- Dogs: Heartworm testing

- Spay/Neuter surgery

- De-wormer

- Flea/Parasite preventative

- Vaccinations

Another consideration to keep in mind: will you utilize one veterinarian or will you work with multiple veterinarians/offices? At Advocates 4 Animals, for example, we work with two different veterinarians for our spay/neuter services and employ a separate veterinarian for our specialty surgeries (i.e. extensive dental work, et cetera) and special cases. Again, what works best for one organization may not be the best fit for another organization. Assess your own agency and decide what will accommodate your needs the most effectively.

Who will you call on evenings and weekends for veterinary emergencies? What qualifies as a medical emergency? Take a moment to jot down your thoughts on these questions. As you move forward in developing your organization, you will develop a system that works best for you. For now, find out who you will utilize for emergency medical care and how you can quickly get the animal in their care when the time comes.

As a side note, keep in mind that when you rescue a pet you are responsible for their care. Even if you grow to have 100+ volunteer foster homes (way to go!), every pet in each foster home is ultimately your responsibility. Your budget needs to reflect adequate funding to support the amount of animals in your program. If a pet comes in with (or develops an issue while in one of your foster homes) a medical issue (i.e. limping leg, an eye in need of removal or special surgery, or any number of other medical issues) it is up to you to provide quality, timely professional veterinary care for each pet. We cannot emphasize enough to stay within your limits. It is tempting to take on more than you can handle; you will receive endless calls, e-mails, and text messages begging for help day after day. But you have to focus on the lives you *can* help. If you say yes to everyone and have too many to care for, you won't be helping anyone. But if you set a specific mission statement and set limits for both yourself and each of your volunteer foster homes, you can make a tremendous difference in the lives of animals in need. Pets who come into your organization will be incredibly lucky to have found their way to you as they recover, become fully vetted and ultimately adopted into well-matched forever homes. You want the experience to be rewarding and positive for everyone involved. Set your limits, stick to them and the rest will fall into place.

Prior to officially starting Advocates 4 Animals in 2003, we spent years volunteering in shelters, pounds and sanctuaries, and working in kennels and veterinarians offices. In the years leading up to our official start, we worked closely with a veterinarian who believed in our work and supported our endeavors. We were not yet a 501(c)3 organization, we weren't even an organization. We were two people who saw a need and wanted to make a positive impact. We were barely twenty-year olds at the time. We carried a stray cat into the veterinarian's office in a laundry basket and set her on the counter as we completed the intake paperwork. We didn't know what was wrong with the cat, but she didn't seem well. While filling out the paperwork, the cat's water broke on the counter and she was rushed into emergency surgery. The memory always leaves us shaking our heads and laughing at our naivety, but the reality was that being at our veterinarian's office at that moment saved the cat's life and she is still with us today (well over a decade later). Her kittens were stillborn and she was unable to birth them on her own. We were at the right place at the right time.

Other cats we brought into our first veterinarian left her looking at us with crazy eyes and shaking her head. One senior cat could hardly stand on her own, and needed countless urgent and significant surgeries. The veterinarian was certain she wouldn't survive, but we wanted to try; a life was at stake. The cat not only survived, but thrived and lived an additional decade. But I digress...

A year after officially starting Advocates 4 Animals, Inc. we moved across state lines for our day jobs. At the time we had a dog (who attacked cats if she saw them) and a dozen rescued cats. With the help of friends and family, we had five vehicles. We loaded up our minimal belongings, separated the pets into each vehicle (we still did not know about pet carriers at this time...the vehicle rides were interesting for each of us as we crossed the state line that day!) and moved away. Our only tear shed was at the loss of our first trusted veterinarian, Theresa. It's been well over a decade now and we still talk about her. She believed in us when no one else did and for that we will always be grateful. We knew moving would bring the challenge of finding a new veterinarian that we both liked and trusted. But we had no idea what a struggle it would be to find just the right one as we settled down, grew our roots and worked around the clock to help our organization grow.

6

NUTS ARE FOR SQUIRRELS

———

IT IS WITHOUT QUESTION that pets within your organization must be spayed/neutered. But what is up for consideration is expanding your organization to provide a spay/neuter clinic or program for the area that your organization serves. If you want to significantly impact local animals, offering low-cost sterilization surgeries in your area is imperative to reaching that goal. If you're intrigued by the idea, keep reading.

Option 1: You can operate a voucher program to assist local pets in need. A voucher program offers discounted or free spay/neuter services via a voucher. There are many options as to how you can operate such a program. Mail vouchers to recipients or meet face-to face with recipients at the time of presenting the voucher.

Things to consider when operating a spay/neuter voucher program:

- What area or zip code will you serve?
- Will the spay/neuter voucher program be tied to income requirements or open to everyone?
- Will you be working with a specific veterinarian for the voucher program? How will you set up your system to work for both your program and for the veterinarians daily work week?
- How many vouchers will you provide each week,

month, year? Do you have a total limit on the number of vouchers you can provide annually?

- What is your cost for each surgery? What cost will you offer to the public? How will you pay the difference? (i.e. if the spay surgery costs $60, but you are offering $10 vouchers – where will you find the extra $50 for every pet that is spayed through this voucher program?)

- Will the vouchers only be for owned pets? Stray pets? Feral cats? Dogs only? Dogs under 10-pounds only? Cats only? *Be specific.*

- Who will schedule the appointment with the voucher? Will the recipient call to make their own appointment? If so, who will they call and how will you ensure that only the spay or neuter are added on your organizations monthly bill (and no additional services)?

- Who will transport the pet(s) to and from the spay/neuter appointments?

- What happens if the pet using the voucher has complications following surgery? Who will cover that cost?

- What happens if the pet being spayed/neutered

through your voucher program is ill and desperately needs medication? Will your organization cover the cost of medication?

• Will you provide a waiver for recipients to sign?

Many additional questions will arise as you begin to plan your program. The above are just a few ideas to get you started. There's a lot to consider prior to establishing such a program!

Option 2: Your organization can expand to open a spay/neuter clinic. While the task seems daunting at first thought, the rewards are countless in opening such a facility. Spay and neuter surgeries save thousands of lives annually. In our own county, we continue to experience a decrease in the intake of felines at our county pound thanks to the implementation of our multitude of viable programs at Advocates 4 Animals. With our county pound having saved a mere 18% of healthy, adoptable felines last year (killing 100% of feral, shy, scared and ill felines), it is imperative to the lives of cats that they stay out of the shelter in the first place.

If your organization is considering opening a

spay/neuter clinic as the non-profit itself or as an extension of your current non-profit organization, we strongly encourage you to contact *Humane Alliance*. When we visited Humane Alliance in Asheville, North Carolina, their new state-of-the-art training facility was nearly complete. Since 1994 the Humane Alliance organization has assisted in training non-profits to expand their programs into high-volume/low-cost spay and neuter clinics around the country. The training they provide to your veterinarians and staff is top-of-the-line, along with the mentorship provided throughout the process of opening your clinic.

A few things to think about as you consider opening a spay/neuter clinic:

- Will you have an income requirement for those who come to your clinic?

- Will you service both cats and dogs on the same day or will you have certain days scheduled only for cats and certain days for dogs only?

- How will you find/hire your veterinarians?

- How will you fund your facility? Equipment?

- Will you be open on weekends only, or regular weekday hours?

- What will you do if your veterinarian leaves or is ill? How will you handle a high-volume of surgeries while he/she is away?

- What grants will you target to assist you with this program?

- What fundraisers will you embark on to assure adequate funding?

- How many surgeries will you need to perform a week in order to keep a viable business model long-term?

- How will you ensure enough funding to cover the salaries of your veterinarians and support staff?

- What will your cost be per animal? What will the cost to the public be per animal? Will you offer vaccinations? For what additional cost? Will you offer microchips (and for what additional cost)? Will you offer FeLv/FIV testing (cats) and/or Heartworm Testing (dogs)?

- You are a spay/neuter clinic, how will you

handle it when someone asks you for medication for their pet? What limits will you set on your services?

- Will you offer flea preventative/treatment (for pets infested with fleas that come into your clinic)? How will you charge?

- Will you offer services for feral cats? If so, will you provide humane traps (rent them out)?

- How many surgeries can you handle (maximum) per day?

- Are there other low-cost sterilization programs in your area? How will your program differ?

Regardless of whether you offer a voucher program or open a spay/neuter clinic, there are a multitude of questions and comments that you will repeatedly hear. We have provided a few of those questions and comments below in order to help you prepare your replies.

- I want my children to see a litter of kittens/ puppies born before I spay/neuter.

- Will altering my pet make them fat?

- Why should I spend money to put my pet under surgery? What are the benefits of spay/neuter?

- At what age should I spay/neuter my pet?

- If my pet is a senior, is it too late to spay/neuter?

- My female dog/cat never goes outside, so there's no reason to have her spayed.

- Will it harm the health of my pet to have them spayed/neutered?

- Will my pet live a shorter life if they are altered?

- Neutering my pet isn't "natural". I don't want to take away my dog/cats "manly-hood".

- My dog is aggressive, will neutering change that behavior?

- Will neutering my male cat stop him from spraying?

- How early can my dog/cat become pregnant?

- Will my dog/cat feel pain during and after surgery?

- Will my animals' behavior change after being altered?

Whether you decide to offer a spay/neuter voucher program or open a spay/neuter clinic, taking time to plan ahead will be key to your success. Maybe a spay/neuter program will be more applicable to your organization down the road. Assessing the above information is just the tip of the iceberg when embarking on such programs. As we talked about before, remember to start small and provide quality service to the pets in your care, your trusted volunteers and your committed adopters. It takes everyone working happily together (within the limits you have set) to make a lasting difference.

7

THE DAILY GRIND

———

DON'T QUIT YOUR DAY JOB. Starting a rescue organization, as with any business, takes years to build into a viable, thriving organism. It's essential that you love what you do or burnout is inevitable. Whether you're starting a for-purpose (i.e. non-profit) or for-profit business, this fact holds true. In real estate they say it's all about: location, location, location. In opening and operating your own business, we say it's all about: passion (for what you do), effective communication, and a work ethic

———

that is second to none (which comes automatically when you have passion for what you do).

One morning, I was running an old rug out to the garbage-can on the curb, trying to beat the garbage truck that was roaring down the street. As I set out the tightly rolled large rug, the driver of the truck hopped out and with a mere peak at the rug started hauling it into the truck for his own personal keeping. I turned to warn him a cat had urinated on the rug, not to mention I hadn't bothered to vacuum it since we were tossing it. He proceeded by asking me what type of business we ran. He said, "What exactly do you do; sell animals?" I explained with as much brevity as possible that we rescued animals, provided spay/neuter and vetting services and found them forever homes. He followed up with, "You must make a ton of money. How do I get into that business?" I couldn't stop my laugher. "I *pay* thousands of dollars to do this every year." I told him. "I don't *make* anything. I do this outside of my regular day job." He looked at me, puzzled and threw the old rug into the back dumpster of the truck and drove off.

While plenty of 501(c)3 organizations grow into

large businesses with paid staff and lush offices, starting any business takes time and in the first several years at least, you will be paying to make your dream a reality – not the other way around.

You are a volunteer of your own organization (at least for the first several years), but don't let that fact fool you into thinking you're not a business. Your attitude will determine the direction of your future. Operate as a professional business; be courteous and kind to your customers (adopters). It cannot be stressed enough how important professional and timely responsiveness is in any business endeavor.

When you receive a call or e-mail, how long will it take you to respond? Set a policy right now. Whether it is an inquiry for adoption or a plea for assistance, will you respond in 48 hours? One week? How will you let those who contact you know how long it will take you to reply?

Furthermore, what will your reply consist of? We provide additional thoughts and insights on screening adopters in Chapter 9. What about those asking for urgent assistance? If your facility is full and unable to take in any additional pets at that time, can you provide any practical resources for the pet in need? If so, what resources will you keep on hand?

Other considerations to keep in mind:

- Who will run your day-to-day operations? Decide who will be in charge of e-mails, who is in charge of the phone and decide the response time.

- Where will your headquarters be located? Will you have open hours?

- As you begin your organization, what hours will you dedicate each day to responding to adoption inquiries, pleas for assistance and other forms of communication? Setting specific times every day is a must. Yes, things will be insanely busy – when you're working a full-time day job, raising a family and caring for your own pets – it's difficult to schedule in additional time for starting a business. But if you really want to start an organization, you must dedicate yourself to it every day. Decide how you will fit in several hours a day to dedicate to growing your organization. Remember, it takes incredibly hard work to start something from scratch. Daily dedication and passion for the cause are essential in creating an organization.

- When will you train new volunteers? Where will training take place?

- Who will answer your hotline (for volunteer foster parents caring for animals in your organization)?

- Who will keep track of your expenses and revenues?

- Who will write thank you letters to donors?

- Who will research grant opportunities? And then...who will write the grants? Who will meet with the grant committees on behalf of your organization?

- Who will create and operate your website?

- Who will create and operate your social media pages?

- Who will complete your annual tax form?

- Do you plan to be part of the Better Business Bureau? Why or why not?

- Who will maintain all of the pet records (i.e. veterinary records)?

- Who will schedule and take pets in your organization to and from your veterinarian(s)?

Of course these are just a few starter questions to get you going. You will discover there are many additional considerations to keep in the forefront of your mind as you embark on your endeavor.

For our organization, we have two individuals running our organization on a full-time basis in addition to countless volunteers and foster homes and an active Board of Directors who keep us growing and constantly moving forward toward our goals. Running numerous viable programs, we instill open hours for several programs such as our Pet Food Pantry, however, we hold our adoptions by appointment often in the volunteer foster homes themselves – or when performing a home check in the potential adopters home. In addition to daily meet and greet sessions, potential adoption appointments, daily veterinary work and appointments, daily feline spay/neuter surgeries and regular check-in's with volunteer foster homes, we spend our days planning fundraiser events, writing grants/meeting with committees, speaking at various engagements, maintaining the website, maintaining adoption inquiries, working with the shelters (daily) to pull death row pets in urgent need, marketing our adoptable pets through quality channels, providing training for new volunteers, responding to more than a hundred daily e-mails and phone calls, keeping our social media outlets up to date, meeting with potential donors, working on multiple TNR/feral cat projects at a time (daily), keeping up to date records of expenses and revenues (lots of paperwork!)...that's just to name a *few* of our daily "to do's". Every day is different and every day brings new challenges, but we love what we do and we wouldn't trade it for the world.

As we stay true to our mission statement, we work endlessly to end the plight of homeless, abused and neglected animals. We each have clear, defined roles within our organization; however, we are ready to jump in at a moment's notice to fill in wherever needed. We utilize each of our strengths to maximize our efforts in maintaining and growing our organization. Some individuals are more suited for certain activities than others; find out what each of your volunteers talents and strengths are and utilize those strengths to enhance your organization.

If you're considering starting an animal rescue or welfare organization and think you'll be rich – stop right now. **Operating a for-purpose (i.e. non-profit) business will not make you rich in your pocket, but if what you're searching for is to feel rich in your heart, you can find that.** It's important to be realistic as you decide whether or not founding and operating an organization is right for you. Do you have the passion and time that it takes to start such an endeavor? Consider potential upcoming life changes: if you're planning to start a family soon and you work a full-time day job, is it the right time to start your organization now or should you put your plan on pause for a year or so while you decide? When you operate an animal rescue/welfare organization, it is inevitable that you will foster pets in your personal home (also keep in mind when a volunteer foster parent suddenly "drops out" the pet will most likely come to your home for a temporary time): are you prepared to deal with the challenges of fostering pets (i.e. scratched furniture, ruined rugs, extra cleaning)? Our prompts and questions are not written to discourage you; rather, they are to prepare you as you consider your new endeavor.

Starting a business of any kind is much like having a baby. Research, planning and strategizing will help you determine if embarking on this endeavor is right for you. Unlike many other businesses, operating an animal rescue adds an extra element of pressure; you have innocent lives depending on and trusting you. Do your homework ahead of time to ensure that you can keep your commitment of helping the animals you rescue.

While still in the first years of starting our organization, we were often asked the same repetitive questions (and statements/judgments) from our day job co-workers:

- So you hang out and play with cats and dogs at night?

- I have a donation I can bring to you. My neighbor has a litter of 9 kittens and the mom is pregnant again. When can I bring them to you to donate?

- Why would you want to work outside of a job you already have?

- Why would you do something that doesn't make any money?

- So you're just doing this until you have children?

- That's a nice hobby.

It's your job to convey what you do to those who inquire. I've never believed in pushy marketing. I'm from the school of thought that your actions truly do speak louder than words. Rather than push your ideals on others, live what you believe and those who are intrigued or who believe the same will inevitably take interest in your efforts and may become inspired to join the cause.

Some days when I publish a new magazine article or blog, or when our posts on social media aren't attracting a high amount of interest or attention, I find myself worried that no one cares about our efforts. But then I look to the extra chair in the office and see four felines cuddled up and purring away lost in a cozy dream and I instantly know that what we're doing does matter. We're not doing this for attention or applause, we're doing this to save lives and we are incredibly grateful for any support we can gain along the way. Two of the cats on the chair are a mom and daughter duo who we rescued together as they stood in the center of the road on a dark stormy night, refusing to move out of the street as our car neared closer. Another is a senior guy who we bottle-fed as an orphaned kitten. He and his brother easily fit into the palm of one petite hand, yet they survived and it has been 14 years since their challenging start. The fourth cat on the chair is one we found hiding beneath a dumpster while exercising. Amy was running while I was riding a bike. We were still three-miles away from home and knowing our only option to save the emaciated cat was to carry him back, I threw off my warm sweatshirt and cradled him in my arms, biking back home and feeling reminiscent of the final scene in the cherished classic movie, E.T.

Some days while operating an animal rescue/welfare organization, you will feel overwhelmed and other days you will feel on top of the world.

In all honesty, there is more bad than good. But we keep working hard and holding onto the hope that our endless efforts will not only make a life changing impact on the individual lives we save, feed, spay/neuter, et cetera – but that our efforts will create a larger impact as a whole, decreasing the number of innocent lives entering the local county shelter (that last year had a mere save rate of 18% of healthy, adoptable cats, and a 0% save rate of shy, feral, scared or sick felines), saving more of the lives that wind up in the pound through no fault of their own, increasing the rate of adoptions and the changing the perception of rescue pets both locally and globally. We keep doing what we do, because we believe in the cause and we believe in us. We know our efforts matter. We know since our start we have saved more than 11,000 lives in need. We know one organization can't save every life in need, but for the ones we can save, we can change their lives in a positive way. For every pet who is spayed/neutered, for example, thousands of additional pets are not born to find themselves in need of help. For every pet adopted into a forever home, a new pet in dire need can be saved. For every pet helped through a pet food pantry program, those very pets can remain in their comfortable homes rather than face being relinquished to a local pound (where they most likely will face certain euthanasia).

When you start a for-purpose organization such as an animal rescue, it's not for the fanfare. While support in the form of donors, adopters, fosters and volunteers is essential, if you keep doing what you believe in, if you work hard every single day (there are no true vacations in animal rescue), if you maintain professional and responsive communications and if you operate as a business (because you are one!), if you've done your homework and created a realistic business plan, the rest will fall into place.

As with anything worthwhile, consistent hard work is a must as you create your animal rescue organization. If you're in a job you don't love and you're simply looking for something new...look long and hard before you leap into rescue. It's not a business for the faint or light-hearted. More often than not we are asked "How can I start a rescue (or non-profit)?" There is just no simple answer. The eager eyes always look back at us, ready for us to provide a magic secret formula. *"You just add a dab of this and a dab of that and poof; you're rich and saving the world."* If that's your image of animal rescue, you have a lot of research and heartbreak ahead of you (sorry to burst your bubble). Whether you're starting a business of creating apps or starting a non-profit endeavor: they all have the same bottom line. Passion, daily hard work, dedication and professionalism (i.e. responsiveness). **I'm convinced there's only one way to be successful in this world and it's through being true to yourself (finding out who you are and what you want from life) and through living your dreams.** The years have taught me that people define success differently. To me, success means happiness. If you can find something that you're happy doing, where you're surrounded by others who make you happy and you can bring happiness to others while doing what you do...to me, that is true success. What is your definition of success?

The daily grind is just that, whether you're working in a cubical or you're embarking on the wild adventures of starting your own organization. The daily grind is filled with endless hard work, there's no way around it. If **you want to create something, the effort must equal that which you**

wish to create. Of course finances are important – essential in fact – to operating your organization as well as to living your life; but the foundation must always be passion. If you find *your* passion, the money will follow. From my earliest memories, I dreamed of being a writer and saving animals. I started telling stories as soon as I could talk (I'm not kidding – my baby book notes my first words as "talks a lot". My parents said once I said my first word I never stopped). I started saving animals as soon as I could walk. But I never dreamed I would really make a living doing what I loved. I thought I *had* to work an ordinary job. I thought I *had* to live life in a certain way. I tried to follow those imaginary *"had to's"* until it nearly took my life.

Find your passion, live your dream. It sounds cliché but it's so true! If your passion is to operate an animal rescue: read this book, make a plan and as the Nike commercials say "Just do it!" But if your passion is taking photographs; do that. If you love animals and you love taking photographs, open a pet photo studio. There are no limits to what you can do. But just remember, regardless of what your gift is and where your passion lies, the daily grind will be waiting for you. Day-to-day hard work is a necessary ingredient to success – or rather, to happiness. You get back that which you give.

8

SETTING STANDARDS

———————

AFTER BEING SENT A FUZZY PHOTO and learning of her urgent plea, we saved a terribly emaciated shelter dog without a name. Unable to stand on her own, we quickly learned that she could neither eat nor drink without assistance. In fact, she couldn't so much as lift her own head off the ground. Her skin clung loosely to her bones, each one poking through her and begging for nourishment. We hadn't been made aware of her condition prior to rescue and when I placed her in my car for the ride back, my heart pounded with worry.

On the drive home, I named her Madie. She rode in the back seat of my Honda car, sprawled out on a fleece blanket. I had three additional dogs with me that day, as we had asked three additional rescues if they would pull a pet from the same shelter so that more lives could be saved. I delivered each of the other three dogs to their respective rescues and raced Madie to our Advocates 4 Animals veterinarian. The prognosis was lousy. In fact I was told, "Don't be surprised if you wake up in the morning and Madie hasn't made it. She's gone far too long without food and water. It's most likely too late." But I held on to hope that a miracle could still happen. Madie had more parasites in her body than our veterinary team had ever witnessed before (However, I was so thankful that she was heartworm negative). She was unable to stand, so she would urinate and defecate on herself. I cradled her head in my hands as I fed her fresh water through a large syringe, followed by a veterinary prescribed food (again through a syringe). Every time she swallowed I was grateful the nourishment was entering her frail body.

When a new pet comes into the rescue, we adhere to a quarantine period for each pet as we work to make sure each one is healthy, tested, and spayed/neutered and vaccinated prior to placing them in their volunteer foster homes within our network of supporters. Madie was in such dire shape that I knew she would remain with me for quite some time. We have a spare bedroom in our house just for cases like Madie. We carried the gaunt beagle-mix into the spare bedroom and worked to provide her with as much comfort as possible. We placed her on a soft extra-large dog bed and covered her body with a bright pink blanket to help her stay warm. We placed several puppy pads in the area surrounding her, knowing that she could not signal when she had to go to the bathroom.

Madie miraculously survived the first night. We continued her regular veterinary visits, daily medications and daily cleaning, watering and feeding routines. It was around-the-clock care. When we were away at work (our day jobs), volunteers came in to care for her. Madie was never alone. Against the odds, after nearly four months of intensive work Madie began to walk, drink and eat on her own. A month later, Madie began playing with toys and interacting with other canines; there was no stopping her now. She made a full recovery after six months and shortly thereafter was adopted into a forever home to call her very own; a home she shared not only with her human family, but with two cats and one other dog.

Looking back, the photos of her journey to recovery still leave me in awe of her transformation. Madie came to us as a full-grown adult dog weighing a mere 12-pounds. Now Madie weighs a healthy 48-pounds (her proper weight) and can out run anyone who tries to race her. She's a beacon of health and happiness and she's found her place in life, cozied up to a family of her own.

It's far from smooth sailing when you operate an animal rescue organization. Just when we think we've seen and heard it all, we are quickly reminded of how wrong we are. There's no way of knowing exactly what to expect day in and day out of operating a viable animal rescue organization; you have to be prepared for pretty much anything!

When we rescued Madie, we had no way of knowing the kind of shape she was in. Whether we receive a call from a local resident/Good Samaritan or when working with a local shelter, we never know until we have the animal in our hands their true condition. More often than not what we're told prior to rescue and what we find when we arrive are two very different stories. Nevertheless, our goal is to save the lives of those in need and with a strong mission statement, a viable organization complete with local qualified/trained volunteers, coupled with a solid new animal intake protocol and standards of care (and of course a trusted veterinarian) you can set yourself up to be ready for whatever comes your way.

A few questions to consider as you consider starting an animal rescue organization:

- What will you do when you rescue an "unadoptable" pet (i.e. a dog who bites or is aggressive, feral cats who cannot be adopted to indoor homes, incredibly fearful cats or dogs who urinate on themselves at the sight of humans – but do not possess the skills to survive as outdoor feral cats)?

- Are you able to commit the time and effort that

it takes to provide around-the-clock care for a rescued pet (whether in your home as a foster pet or in your facility)? If you work a full-time job, who will provide constant care to special needs pets (in need of specialized rehabilitation)?

- How will you assess the behavior of each adoptable pet in your organization once they are healthy and fully vetted? How can you be sure that the pet does well with small children? Other dogs? Other cats?

- What will your protocol be for the intake of a new animal? Where will they stay? Who will care for them? What veterinary care will be provided (and how quickly)?

- Will you have the funds to cover emergency medical costs for new rescue animals (i.e. surgeries, medications, et cetera)?

While it's imperative to set specific standards and protocol for your organization, it is equally important to listen to your intuition. You know that little voice in the back of your head; that feeling you get right in the center of your gut; that's your intuition communicating to you. It's up to you to pay attention.

When we received a call to save five adult cats living outside of an apartment complex that sat next to a busy interstate, the senior citizen on the other end of the line told us that she had contacted more than 100 rescues and everyone had either A) ignored her calls and emails (providing no reply or acknowledgement whatsoever) or B) a few of them had returned her requests for help, simply to say "no, we cannot help." They offered no resources, solutions or advice. So when we said yes at Advocates 4 Animals, Jane was nearly jumping for joy. The apartment manager planned to trap and kill any cats in the area at the end of the week. We got to work quickly and soon found that what Jane thought were five cats turned into more than 60. Yes, you read that right. It took us nearly three years to successfully catch, spay/neuter, place in foster homes and adopt all 60 cats: but with persistence and a lot of hard work we saved them all. The cats at the complex were regularly chased, shot at (90% of them had BB's surgically removed from beneath their skin once rescued) and tormented. Jane provided one insulated hut and daily food and water for the cats in the area as we worked to save each one. During the first year of work, one of the cats was a large burly brown tiger. He lunged at the cage and hissed with fury. His head was large and his eyes angry for all that he had endured while trying his best to survive the abuse, torment and loneliness of being a stray. Many of the cats rescued during this project were so badly damaged that they required months of one-on-one therapy with an experienced volunteer, in order to be rehabilitated socially and emotionally and prepared for adoption.

One particular large male tiger cat from this rescue was very angry. He was neutered by our Advocates 4 Animals veterinarian and it was discovered at that time that his back leg had been previously broken (most likely hit by a moving vehicle) and had healed as best as it could on its own without the intervention of medical care (or proper nutrition for that matter). The result was that he dragged his back leg behind him whenever he moved.

As the cat recovered from surgery in his large crate lined with plush blankets and full food and water bowls, anytime we came near him he would lung forward in an attempt to swat at us. Our veterinarian strongly recommended that we release him to a managed feral cat colony but my gut said otherwise. As our veterinarian went home for the night I walked up to the angry cat and sat on a stool, hands in my lap, eyes low to the ground. As the cat inevitably lunged towards the front of the cage, I began softly talking. To any outsider, I am sure I looked like a crazy person at that moment; but I didn't care. My intuition told me to pry a bit further; to see if the mad cat might be workable. Truly feral cats will typically hide in the back of their cages and want nothing to do with you. But this guy was intensely irate which told me he longed for a healthy interaction with humans; he just didn't know how to get there. As I sat on the stool talking to the cat (mostly to myself) eventually he stopped lunging and hissing and sat quietly near the door of the cage. I was careful not to make eye contact while he watched me sitting on the stool, babbling away. After a bit of time I just sat in silence; the cat mirrored me as he did the same. I slowly dared to raise my eyes to meet his in a gentle way and said, "You're not feral, you're just scared. Give me some sort of sign that you're not feral...we'll work to rehabilitate you if you want the help." Almost immediately the mad cat let out a sweet innocent meow as he lowered his head, rubbing against the front door. I had been given a sign and knew instinctively that my gut had been right all along. We named him Garth and I began fostering him, giving our spare bedroom to him as he began his journey to recovery.

Garth's rehabilitation was far from a walk in the park. As the only individual *allowed* to enter his room, I knew to wear full pants and thick long-sleeve shirts when I came to visit. Garth would lunge at me in anger, hisses escaping his mouth as he desperately tried to protect himself from his own unthinkable past. My hands were tucked away into the sleeves of my sweatshirt or he would viciously attack, drawing blood each time. If it sounds awful, it was. But I knew each time I entered, that it was a chance for progress. I know working with an attack cat sounds crazy, but my hunch told me loud and clear that with patience and dedication Garth would make a full recovery. I persisted in my efforts, although to anyone on the outside those very efforts may have seemed hopeless. Each time I entered I sat near the door or in a corner of the room, hands tucked inside of my shirt sleeves, eyes looking down and sitting quietly. My goal was for Garth to simply get used to a human being in the room with him and realizing that he didn't need to be terrified; realizing that not all humans would harm him.

It worked. After several months, Garth stopped lunging towards me. I still wore long sleeves and pants, but he was no longer coming after me. He allowed me to enter his room and slowly I inched my hands from out of my sleeves. At the sight of my hands Garth reverted back to his attacks. Again it was a slow, gradual process. But in time I could sit with my hands fully exposed, in my lap and Garth was relaxed.

Still he wouldn't allow anyone but me into his room. He watched me fill his food and water bowls and clean his litter box. Eventually I began talking or reading to him as I sat in his room to visit. Next I added a radio, keeping it playing on a quiet volume 24/7 so that he could get used to both male and female voices and various sounds; I wanted him to realize that the sound of human voices were no longer a cause for panic (or attack).

The day Garth walked up to me as I sat against

the door reading aloud, I couldn't help but hold my breath. He rubbed me and then proceeded to curl up in my lap as if that is what he had always done. I had no doubt that he had once curled up in the same way earlier in his life, most likely when he was a young kitten with a home (before being dumped and left to fend for himself). Once he sat on my lap and began to purr, his social and emotional rehabilitation took off. Now he held his tail high when I entered the room. He was allowing other quiet and calm visitors. With a bit more time, Garth had enough confidence to leave his room and meet my cats and dogs and he did great with everyone; he even learned to play. His recovery was nothing short of miraculous. It took less than a year for Garth to make a full recovery and when he did, he was adopted into the most wonderful forever home of his dreams. Garth's story has been featured in CAT FANCY magazine since his adoption and we receive a holiday card from Garth and his family every year.

What will you do when you rescue a pet within your organization and then learn that he/she is aggressive? Possibly a feral cat? A cat/dog who bites? What plan of action will you take? Do you have a trusted professional dog trainer who you will work with to assist in special cases?

It is inevitable when operating an animal rescue you will come across a variety of pets who are in need of intensive one-on-one social and emotional rehabilitation. One fact that is commonly overlooked is ENVIRONMENT. **The environment in which the pet is living can completely alter his/her temperament and personality.**

We are inundated with daily pleas for help in the following situations:

- Pet guardians who state their dog has nipped or bitten their child (often we come to learn it is because the child was harming the dog in some way)

- "Feral" cats needing rescue—but in reality the cats are just scared or shy

- Cats with spraying or urination issues (often because the cat is not altered, or the introduction of a new dog, baby or significant other has recently occurred or some other major life altering event)

- Cats not using the litter box (most often this is due to a health issue)

- Dogs or cats being "destructive" (most often this happens due to a lack of socialization/exercise – being "bored")

- Chained dogs who have become aggressive (most often the "aggression" is coming from frustration from lack of socialization, et cetera)

Placing the pet in an appropriate environment can almost always remedy any situation. All too often pet guardians are not willing to look at what *they* can do to correct the issues at hand, rather, they prefer to "pass the buck" and have someone else handle the problem. While a rescue organization is not a pet training facility, there are ways we can assist pet guardians in providing or locating the proper home environment for their pet(s).

While out for a walk with my own three dogs last night, I hoped for a relaxing stroll through the neighborhood, allowing me to unwind from a long stressful day of work. As we turned the corner and turned down the next street in our path, I witnessed a young girl screaming and running towards a white Labrador-mixed dog. The dog tucked her tail and squatted in a nearby front yard with a look of fear. The young girl reached the dog and proceeded to cruelly jab her ribs several times; a moment later she sat next to the dog hugging her. Clearly the dog had run down the street from her home: a home the family had just moved to not more than a week earlier. As we continued walking in the direction of the young girl and her dog, another individual approached the dog. She was older than the young girl, most likely a teenager and as she approached, the dog nearly wet herself. As the younger child had done, the older girl hit the dog twice and screamed at her to never run away again. The two girls placed the dog on a leash and dragged her back to their home just three doors down; all the while, screaming at the dog that she was terrible and to never run away again.

My heart ached. How could they hit their dog? Did they really think that was helping the dog to understand why they were so upset? The dog's tail remained tucked beneath her, pressed against her stomach and she quivered in terror. Of course I wanted to run across the street to the dog, but I was limited because of walking my own three dogs. As I continued walking in their direction on the cul-de-sac street, I heard the girls tell themselves that they would lock the dog in a room when they got inside, so that she would be punished. Everything about the situation was wrong and it nearly killed me not to get involved. The dog couldn't win. I couldn't take the dog, it wasn't mine. The dog couldn't apologize; she couldn't explain to the children or the family that she had just been scared and she was sorry.

Two weeks later, the family placed a hand written sign in their lawn "FREE DOG."

Environment is a key element to happiness. When I saw the sign in the yard, I knew the dog would clearly be happier in a different environment; an environment that provided unconditional love and proper positive reinforcement training. But placing a "FREE PET" sign or ad is just asking for trouble (More on this in the following chapter covering pet adoption).

When it comes to drafting and ultimately to implementing the protocols and standards of care for your animal rescue organization, be sure to consider how you will handle special circumstances such as those mentioned in this chapter.

CHAPTER 8 CHALLENGE:

- Revisit this chapter and spend time answering the bullet-point questions.

- Draft your new pet intake protocol (i.e. create a checklist of items to perform upon intake)

- Draft your Standards of Care (i.e. What type of rehabilitation efforts will your organization provide to all animals in your care – whether in a facility or in volunteer foster homes? For example, will you offer one-on-one social/ emotional rehabilitation services? Who will provide this service? Are they experienced in this area?)

- How will you respond to pleas from pet guardians who wish to give up their pets due to what they view as a "behavior issue"?

- If you agree to work on a rescue project that claims to have five cats, but turns out to have 60+ cats – are you equipped to handle the responsibilities of such a large project?

- If your organization works with dogs and you receive a plea to help a dog who has bitten a child, will your organization take in such a pet? If so, what services will you provide prior to placing this pet up for adoption? If not, what resources will you offer to the pet guardian?

9

OPT TO ADOPT

————

IT SHOULD GO WITHOUT SAYING that adoptions are essential to the viability of your organization. Without adoptions, you would quickly run out of space for additional rescues. Adoptions must be a priority within your organization if you are going to remain active on the rescue front. The more qualified forever homes you locate for the pets within your rescue organization, the more pets you can save: pets that are urgently waiting for assistance and who often have limited time on their side.

When we first started Advocates 4 Animals, we offered free adoptions. Adopters completed an application and interview process and we performed a home check prior to the adoption, we just omitted the adoption fee thinking we could create a high number of adoptions and save more lives. If adopters wanted to donate we welcomed it, but we didn't make it mandatory at the time. But it wasn't so easy. Despite our home-checks and application process, the absence of an adoption fee eventually resulted in a high-rate of return. Without the adoption fee, many of those who were opting to adopt (for free) did not feel the need to commit. There are a whole host of reasons to never adopt out a pet for "FREE", but it still astonishes me to think that requiring something as simple as an adoption fee can deter those potential adopters who are not willing to make a lifelong commitment. This same phenomenon occurred when we offered "adoption specials" (i.e. reduced adoption fees) as well. There is a bit of a science behind finding the proper adoption fee and adoption protocol, to ensure that the rescued pets in your organizations care are adopted to qualified and committed homes.

Close to 90% of our "FREE" adoptions ended up as returns. Approximately 50% of the pet's adoption for an extremely reduced fee (i.e. $25) also faced return. Establishing an appropriate adoption fee is essential to the viability of your organization. (Note: We have always required that pets adopted through our organization be returned to us in the event the adopters cannot keep their commitment. We do this to ensure that once we rescue a pet, they will be safe and properly cared for, for the duration of their life).

Below you will find a list of (a few of) the reasons never to adopt a pet for FREE:

- Free pet ads can attract Class B Dealers (i.e. individuals who find free pets and sell those very pets to testing labs for a fee)

- Free pet ads can attract those involved in dog fighting (i.e. for fighting dogs, for bait animals, et cetera— often times individuals will pose as a family or as a loving adopter)

- Free pet ads can attract those who are "spur of the moment" and often not committed to the long-term care of the pet they are adopting (or unable to afford regular pet care, veterinary visits, et cetera).

- "Flipping" of pets – especially with dogs – is an all too frequent occurrence; free pet ads (i.e. craigslist) often encourage this underground "business".

It is imperative to establish an appropriate adoption fee(s) for the pets in your organization. While doing a background check/questionnaire/ interview and home-check are also important, establishing a proper fee can make all of the difference in your search to find qualified adopters.

Additional benefits to establishing a proper adoption fee:

- Adoption fees help to offset some of the standard veterinary costs your organization incurs for each pet. (*For example, if your organization spends an average of $175 per cat to health check, spay/neuter, vaccinate, de-worm, FIV/FeLV and provide a flea and parasite preventative – your adoption fee of $80 will only cover a portion of your fees. Keep in mind, the adoption fee is NOT in place to cover what you have spent. In many cases you will spend a great deal more than the "standard" amount- as many pets come in to rescue needing additional surgeries, medications and other care. It is not up to the adopter to cover all of your veterinary fees. It is up to you to think outside of the box and figure out how you will afford veterinary fees for every pet you rescue – even if that pet happens to never find a qualified adopter*).

- Adoption fee's help in locating qualified potential adopters. By assessing an appropriate adoption fee, adopters are reminded that pets are a long-term commitment and will require ongoing veterinary care (and additional costs) throughout the duration of their life.

Eliminating "same day adoptions" is another way to increase the likelihood of locating committed forever homes for every pet. At Advocates 4 Animals, we require that all potential adopters complete our online adoption application as the first step. The adoption application is then assessed. We want to ensure the potential adopter and the pet they are interested in are a good match for one another (i.e. if the pet needs a calm, quiet home, we want to be sure the potential adopters home environment matches this criteria prior to moving forward).

We assess the adoption application and then make contact with the potential adopter(s) to discuss any concerns or questions they may have about the adoption process or about their potential new pet. Taking this step allows us to get to know each adopter and help make the best fit for both the human adopters and the pet(s). In addition, waiting 24 hours (minimum) prior to the adoption allows the adopters to take additional time to think about the adoption, address concerns they may have, et cetera.

What will your screening process look like? What questions do you feel are essential on your adoption application? How will you handle the actual adoption? Will you provide copies of veterinary records and the pets file on adoption day? What other information/resources will you provide to adopters? When and how will you schedule adoptions? Will they be held in the foster home (or your facility) or in the adopter's home? What are the pros and cons you can think of for each option? Will you have open hours or will adoptions be schedule by appointment only? If adoptions are scheduled only via appointment, how timely can you schedule and confirm the appointment(s)? Remember timing is everything! There are thousands of pets in need of loving homes. Your rate of responsiveness will be an important factor in determining your overall annual adoption rates.

Will you discuss your return policy with every adopter? What is your return policy? Do you require that pets adopted through your organization only be returned to *you* if the adoption does not work out for any reason? Do you have any resources in place to assist with issues that may arise after the adoption?

Nathan Winograd of the *No Kill Advocacy Center* discusses the necessity of implementing a comprehensive adoption program within your organization. A comprehensive adoption program includes more convenient public access hours (especially evening and weekend hours).

While returns are always difficult for both the rescue organization (where will you place the returned pet?) and for the pet (it is very difficult on pets to switch environments), you must be prepare for the return of an adopted pet. Below we have provided a list of the top reasons pets have been returned. Please ask your potential adopters to take these elements into consideration when contemplating adopting a new pet.

- Divorce/Couple splitting up
- Allergies
- Pregnancy/New baby
- Marriage
- Moving
- Death of a family member
- Can't afford pet food (temporary financial hardship)

- The pet doesn't fit with the family's lifestyle (i.e. active household/shy pet)

- Ill cat (i.e. can't afford veterinary care)

- Pet nibbles or bites a family member

- Pet isn't house trained or stops using the litter-box

- Pet can't get along with the other pets in the household

- New job (not at home as many hours)

- Behavior issues (i.e. cat jumps on kitchen counters, puppy is chewing on household items)

While it's impossible to completely eliminate returns, you can drastically reduce the rate of returns and increase the number of quality adopters by instilling an appropriate screening process, adoption fee and adoption process. Discussing the possibility of the above mentioned issues with potential adopters is a must, as you are trusting the adopter(s) with a pet you have worked hard to save, provide veterinary care for and to place him/her in a well-matched home.

Keep in mind that you may not personally connect to every adopter who comes your way. When you adopt hundreds or thousands of pets from your organization annually, you will meet a vast array of personalities. Adopters will come from a variety of backgrounds (including varying religious and political views) and it is important to realize that you are looking for a qualified match between the potential adopter(s) and the pet(s). There will be some adopters with whom you will instantly bond and ultimately become lifelong friends. Others may leave you surprised at times, but it is important to remember what matters is not your potential friendship with the adopter(s), but the assessment of the match between the adopter and the pet they are adopting. Providing your expertise in finding a well-matched pet for your adopters is a valued service provided by your organization. While some adopters will come to you knowing that they want a specific adoptable pet, others will gladly accept guidance in finding the best fit for their home and for their lifestyle.

We've had adopters come and literally lay down on the floor, waiting to see what cat comes to them first and that is how they want to decide *who* to adopt. We've had adopters who take five hours to decide between two cats and other adopters who feel instantly connected to a pet from seeing one photo online. We've had adopters who are first time pet owners and others who will cry as they reminisce and bring out a pile of photo albums featuring their former pets who have since passed away.

Ultimately adoption is the goal of your organization. If adoptions weren't needed, rescues wouldn't be necessary. Unfortunately, that is still the reality we live in. Adoptions are needed, *desperately*. Qualified, committed homes are in high-demand. The more qualified adopters you can secure for the pets in your organization, the more lives you can adequately save. It is up to you to map out a plan as you work towards obtaining those loyal adopters and building your organization one action at a time.

CHAPTER 9 CHALLENGE:

- How will you determine your adoption fee(s)?

- How will you screen adopters to ensure they are a qualified potential home for the particular pet they are interested in?

- Will you adopt to those who rent or only home-owners?

- Will you ask for references on your adoption application and check those references prior to moving forward with the adoption?

- Will you have an age requirement for adoption?

- Will you do a home-check of the potential adopters home, prior to adoption?

- What adoption policies will you have in place?

- Design a draft of your future adoption contract.

- How will you handle returns? Where will the pet go when they are returned? Will you pick up the pet from their home or will you have the adopter bring the pet they are returning to you? Think about the pros and cons of each method.

- Will you attend adoption events? Why or why not?

- How will you determine if the adoption match is right for both the human adopters and for the pet?

- What programs/resources will you provide to adopters who contact you (after the adoption) with behavior related issues?

- Will you follow-up with adopters at a future date? If so, how frequently do you plan on doing so?

- Talk with other No Kill rescue/adoption organizations in your state. How many pets do they adopt annually? What is their return rate? What are the top reasons for returns within their own organizations? What are their adoption policies and procedures?

10

WE ARE A FAMILY

———

"YOU MUST KNOW THE MAGIC FORMULA!" We're often told. "It's hard to adopt cats, especially adult ones. But somehow you find the greatest homes!" I'll let you in on a little secret right now, *there is no secret*. We work hard, we're devoted to our work and we care about the animals we've committed ourselves to helping. That's it. Sound simple? It's not and that's the part no one wants to hear. The truth is, we find great homes for the pets in our care because we work around-the-

———

clock to promote every pet; because we get to know each pet's personality and help to make proper matches between the human adopters and the rescue pets. We find great homes because we are constantly thinking outside of the box and finding new ways to market our adoptable pets to qualified homes. We find great homes for adult, senior and special needs pets because we won't give up on them. When we rescue them we vow to help them find *their* place in life; a place filled with love, safety and happiness. It's not sheer luck that strikes, it's persistence and hard work.

But, if you're looking for an easy solution to finding great adopters, I do have one to share with you...reply to your phone calls and emails! You wouldn't believe how many rescue organizations don't reply at all. Am I serious? Very. I can't begin to tell you how many adopters we have who tell us they have contacted ten or more rescue organizations in searching for their next pet, only to receive no reply or put off. How are they put off? We've heard that if they get a reply at all, often the reply comes a week (or a month) later and is unfriendly. All too often we're told that if the potential adopters have received a reply, the reply says that the individual operating the rescue is "busy" but will get back to them at a more convenient time. Or the reply sends the potential adopter jumping through needless hoops, all in what seems like an effort to stall the adopter.

In the adopter's pursuit of finding a new pet to add to their home, they continue their search and when they find us, we are told tales of headaches and heartaches. Why did they come to us? Because we were friendly and we responded quickly. And when they come to us we want the potential adopter to have a great experience. **Our hope is that when they adopt from us that they will spread the word of their experience to friends, family and co-workers and they too will opt to adopt a rescue pet.** If their friends and family adopt through our organization- great! If they adopt through a local shelter or other rescue that's great too! Our goal is to provide a positive experience so that adopters will become lifelong advocates of rescue pets; this is the way to help more pets in need.

If you're in search of a magic formula, know that the first required ingredient is responsiveness. Provide courtesy and helpful responses to e-mails and phone calls within 48 hours. If it's just you operating the organization at the start, instill a back-up plan (individual) who can respond to e-mails and check your social media pages in your absence. Remember, you are operating a business and it's important to be professional and timely with your communications.

Businesses are built on habits and leadership. Even when you're first starting out, the tendencies you establish will ultimately impact your organization. Your habits shape your leadership style and as more individuals step-up to volunteer and/or be employed by your organization, the more the intricacies of your patterns will show through in the output of your business and your work.

How can you be reached?

We were late to the game when it came to Facebook. I admit it was a personal matter of contention. I didn't want to join the Facebook world, it seemed too intrusive. In 2010 I finally caved. Co-workers (at my day job) constantly talked about Facebook and what they read on the site the night before. I felt out of the loop and while

I wasn't too concerned personally, as they gossiped over lunch about various posts on the social media site, I let my mind drift and began to explore the possibilities of helping animals in need through such a medium. As 2010 arrived, we joined millions of people in the world of Facebook and set up a page for Advocates 4 Animals; and I'm so glad we did. Facebook has created an additional way for us to reach supporters we may have never found. I've heard rumors that many businesses (for-profit and non-profit alike) buy "likes" to increase their exposure. Others buy ads. We've grown organically. We utilize social media as a free source of advertising our work. Advocates 4 Animals doesn't have the most followers of any organization, but because we have grown our base of supporters organically, our followers are those who truly support our work and who are highly involved in our efforts to save lives. Isn't that the type of supporter we want?

Currently, there are a numerous social media sites from YouTube to Pinterest and everything in between. We see start-up businesses (and animal rescues/welfare organizations) try to be a part of every type of social media and we have yet to see that strategy pay off. Our philosophy has always been to pick one or two social media sites and devote our time to those. Ultimately, the choice is yours; but we recommend finding a handful of social media sources that you enjoy utilizing and keep your organization's page up to date so you can spread the word about the work that you're doing and your future goals. Focus is the key. **And on the topic of focus...don't let social media get in the way of your actual work.** It's easy to get sucked into the realm of tech-world, but don't let that happen to you. Stay active in the work that you do, stay true to your mission statement. **Save lives, do good work and get the word out.** But don't spend the majority of your time on social media getting caught up in other posts or communications. Use social media for the free exposure it provides and stay grounded in your work. After all, your work is your passion and you don't want to miss out on living in reality when there is so much to do!

In addition to being active on social media sites we recommend working with a web-designer to create a clean user-friendly website. Spend a significant amount of time reviewing other websites both in your area and in other areas of business. If you're starting an animal rescue, you can still find bits and pieces of a site that you find intriguing on a site for say, clothes. You never know until you look. Research, research, research. And...as a note of caution, DO NOT COPY one organization's site or content. I repeat, DO NOT COPY another organization's website or content. I can't tell you how often I see this: from the name of an organization to the website design and copy- it's tacky and it's unoriginal. Your organization should reflect *your* mission statement and your organization's work. Not someone else's. You will certainly grab bits and pieces of ideas from various sites throughout your months of research, but keep it at that. Find a way to make your website unique to *your* organization. It's time to think outside of the box; put your thinking caps on!

One more note in regard to responsiveness and communications: be sure to include your organization's contact form (and or e-mail, phone number and address) clearly on the front page of your web-site. You can have a beautiful website but if your contact information is difficult to find you will never secure clients (i.e. potential adopters).

Community Involvement

Maintaining focus on your day-to-day operations (and your mission statement) is essential to the viability of your organization. However, it is also important to come out of your bubble every once and awhile and open your eyes to the events in your own local community. What exactly do I mean? You work hard, you're saving the lives of innocent animals in need and you've established a solid brand. Your community knows about the local work you are doing and the difference you are creating; but do you know what other businesses and organizations are working toward in your community? Take some time to visit local businesses and other non-profit organizations; you never know when an opportunity for collaboration may be presented. Now I'm not saying go to every business in town and solicit your for purpose (i.e. non-profit) organization- although you certainly can do that if you wish. But what I'm proposing is to simply meet the people in your town. Get to know each other. It may sound old-fashioned but what ever happened to slowing down to simply say hello? *The more people we know, the more we can grow.* When we take time to come out of our bubble of seclusion and learn about our own town, the effort can go a long way. Getting to know the individuals who operate other businesses in your area can prove beneficial in the long-run. You never know when a local business may want to partner with a non-profit organization to assist in raising awareness or funds. You never know when the owner of a local business may be looking for her next pet. We're all quick to establish online friendships as we surf the web, but what about good-old friendships down the street? Gaining the support of your communities local businesses can go a long way in supporting your mission of helping animals in need. Believe me, when you're operating an animal rescue organization you will be inundated with urgent pleas and you'll need all of the support (volunteers and funding) that you can get.

For years, Advocates 4 Animals has held an annual Car & Dog Wash fundraiser in the same town. While it's not a large fundraiser, it invites the public to come out and meet some of our volunteers and supporters and gives the community a chance to learn more about our organization and the work we are doing. Every year we partner with a local county program that works with prisoners to assist in providing them the skills needed to transition from prison to life outside of the concrete walls. Some years we work with the women's program, others we work with the men's. Approximately a dozen prisoners come to volunteer at our event as their supervisors stand watch along the sidelines. Their task is to wash the cars that come to our fundraising event. For many of these men and women, it is their first time being outside of the barbed wire fence in years. We've seen some individuals break down in tears of happiness and others share their stories with us as they soak the next car in with giant soap suds. At the end of the day we all gather together in a circle and we thank them for their volunteer work with us. We share a story or two of animals that our organization has helped that year and we stress the importance of working together as a community to improve the lives of animals (and of all living beings) through positive actions. Some nod their heads; others have a distant look in their eyes knowing they will soon be heading back to prison, once again sealed away behind those barbed wire fences. We provide them with free candy bars and sodas as they volunteer their time with us and inevitably during every end of the day speech, many of the individuals are scarfing down multiple candy bars and sodas before that privilege is gone. When the speech is over, we sit and talk for a few minutes longer and some offer to share comments and feedback on the day's experience. Afterwards, they walk single-file into a passenger van with windows lined with bars; leaving behind their empty candy bar wrappers and a few memories we hope might be enough to inspire them as they work toward their individual release dates. We never know what happens to each of them as they continue their lives; we wish each one of them the best and sincerely thank them for their efforts at our fundraiser.

It's our smallest fundraiser of the year, but it's a significant one that leaves an imprint on each of our souls. At the end of the day we know that we came together- *rich, poor, white, black, prisoned and free*- to create a kinder, stronger community.

One year during this particular fundraiser event, a man in his mid-twenties shared his story with us. We were warned by the supervisors that the prisoners will often say anything they can think of to grab sympathy and to make you believe they are inherently good. I couldn't help but wonder, *but aren't we all inherently good?* Isn't it our environment, our experiences and ultimately our choices that define us? The young man seemed incredibly sincere and explained his tough childhood filled with drugs, weapons and violence. His guardians had him out "selling" at age 8. I was grateful he shared his story with us and I watched as his eyes filled up with heavy tears he tried desperately not to shed. But his next words were what really stuck with me. "I never knew people did things like this. I never knew people worked for free to help other lives." I was speechless. He went on to tell us about a dog he once had and how he never knew what happened to him and he ended our conversation by considering being a dog-trainer when he was free again. I have no idea whether or not he was ever released or became a dog trainer; I couldn't even tell you his first name. But what I do know is that because of our small community fundraiser that day, he and a dozen or so other men had an opportunity to see the world from a new perspective.

While adequate funding and a focus on your

goal are essential to the viability of your organization, being aware and involved in your local community is an enriching and rewarding experience in a myriad of ways.

CHAPTER 10 CHALLENGE:

- Will you respond to all e-mails and phone calls within 48 hours?

- Who is your "back-up" in case of illness, etc.? (i.e. to respond to adoption inquiries, et cetera)

- What modes of communication will you employ? Phone number? Email(s)? Web-site? Social Media?

- Will you hire a company to create/design your website? What elements do you feel are necessary on your organization's website? How much will it cost to build your site? How will you drive traffic to your site?

- How will you gain community support?

- What ideas do you have for working collaboratively with other non-profits or businesses in your area?

ADVOCATING FOR COMMITMENT

———

"WE ARE NO LONGER ABLE TO KEEP OUR PET. We considered breeding him so we never had him altered. He bit our child, but he is really a great dog. He just needs a home without children. Can you take him? We need to have him gone before dinner tonight." This is verbatim an e-mail we received today at Advocates 4 Animals. We receive countless such emails on a daily basis and the objectivity of it

tends to wear on you day in and day out. While we hustle to rescue death row (shelter) pets before it's too late and stray animals who have nearly given up their will to live, coming back to the office with a computer screen filled with owner surrender pleas can leave you feeling hopeless in your efforts.

Of course, there are endless questions that buzz through our minds as we read one plea after the next. More often than not, the individual asking for immediate assistance doesn't bother to tell us their location or any pertinent details such as how old the pet is or if he/she has health issues, et cetera. It now seems common place for many individuals to "pass off" their misbehaving pets to an animal rescue organization rather than seeking the help of a professional trainer or behaviorist. The "that's just not convenient" mentality seems to have reached epidemic proportions and is costing thousands of pets their own innocent lives every year.

When a pet guardian is desperate to give away their pet due to a behavior issue, how can the pet really win? Shelters and rescue organizations across the country are filled to maximum capacity on a daily basis. Those same organizations have dozens or hundreds of pets in their care: how can they possibly provide special training and assistance to dogs who have bitten or cats who refuse to use the litter-box? In real estate, realtors must disclose what they know about the home they are selling. If a crime occurred in the home, for example, they must disclose that fact to potential buyers. In animal rescue/adoption, you are trusted to do the same. If an animal in your organization has bitten someone or has litter-box issues that you are aware of, you must disclose the issue to potential adopters. And where will you find an adopter for a dog who bites or a cat who sprays? You won't. If you don't disclose the behaviors you know about (or have learned while fostering) with the pets you have available for adoption, the pet will wind up in a home that will return him or worse, pass him off to someone else without telling them what *they* know. And that's not fair to anyone involved. So what's the answer? That is up to you. Will your organization work with these cases? If not, what viable resources will you provide to those asking for assistance?

Most rescue organizations contain a clause within their adoption contracts stating if the adoption does not work out for any reason, at any time, the adopter will return the adopted pet to their organization (not given away to another home, sold, or turned into a shelter). The reason for such a clause is to keep the animal safe. Prior to coming to an animal rescue organization, most pets have suffered a traumatic or neglectful past to some degree. When a pet is welcomed into a rescue organization, while it's imperative to set a comprehensive adoption protocol in place and to stress to adopters that the goal is find committed, forever homes for each pet within your organization, the only way to ensure that a pet remains safe for his/her lifetime is to provide the return clause in your adoption contract.

Whether it's been a month or ten years, when an adopter of a pet from your organization contacts you to return the pet, how will you respond? What will be your protocol for a return request?

Some organizations ask those wishing to "return" a pet if they would be willing to foster the pet for the organization while a new home is located. In this situation you must assess whether or not the current environment is safe for the pet. While the home may have been an excellent fit at the time of adoption, home life may have changed dramatically and the pet must be re-located to a new environment as soon as possible.

Discuss the reason for return with your adopters. Is it because of a divorce or death in the family and the home environment has changed? Or is it because the family hit an unexpected financial hardship and cannot afford pet food? Discovering the reason for return can provide helpful clues and insight into the situation to offer realistic solutions.

Did you know that dogs turned into shelters and pounds are between eight months of age and two years-old? It just so happens it is between those ages when dogs have outgrown that "cute puppy look" and are the most destructive (and also at their highest energy). Untrained dogs may urinate on the floor and/or chew on expensive furniture and shoes, not realizing they are doing any harm. While it's true that some dogs require more training than others, training the humans in the home is just as- if not more- important to reaching the goal of a harmonious home. Television star Cesar Millan has been dubbed "The Dog Whisperer" as he practices and teaches his canine training methods (in addition to stressing the importance of training the canine guardians). Millan's books, DVD's and other helpful materials are found online or at your local book store. His training methods can be helpful to understand and utilize when operating an animal rescue organization.

For cats who develop litter-box issues, it's important to note a whole host of factors may be at play in these situations. Has the cat in question (i.e. the cat the guardian wants to return because of this issue) been checked by a veterinarian for this very issue? It is very possible that the feline may be suffering from a Urinary Tract Infection or other health issue. If all health issues are ruled out by the adopter's veterinarian, what type of litter-box is the cat using? Has the guardian recently switched the type of litter or style of litter-box? Has the litter-box location recently been changed? Have there been environmental changes recently (i.e. addition of a new member to the household, a new pet, moving to a new home, etc.)? Have the adopters tried using Feliway? Have they moved the location of the litter-box to a more secluded location (away from the washer/dryer and away from the furnace—which can make loud noises and scare the cat from using the litter box)? Have the adopters tried Dr. Elsey's Precious Cat Litter (a litter that is guaranteed to solve litter box issues)? You get the idea. There are plenty of questions to ask when an adopter states they want to return their pet. When you embark on an open-dialogue with the adopter and begin to learn more about their current situation, you may be able to better understand how to assist the pet. A return may not be necessary if something in the environment is tweaked to correct the issue causing concern.

Thinking back to Chapter 9 when we discussed the protocol development for the screening of potential adopters, keep in mind that while you cannot prevent a return from *ever* happening within your organization, you can implement a screening process that works for your organization; one that works to find qualified and committed adopters for the pets in your care.

Years ago when we received a call regarding two adult cats that a guardian wished to surrender; we conversed with the guardian to inquire why she wanted to surrender her cats. The cats were each nearly 10 years old and the woman on the line claimed the cats had urinated on her bed. She said she wouldn't tolerate it and if we didn't take them in she would have them euthanized at the veterinarian's office the next day. We offered to come to her home to assess the situation and provide further guidance as to how she could keep the cats with her and live harmoniously. Upon arrival, the woman raced around her house disappearing behind piles of boxes and other items, ranting and raving, mostly to herself about how she could not believe her cats would do this to her. "How could they hurt *me* like this?" She bellowed. The woman was so upset her cats had urinated on her bed that she wasn't willing to take a moment to assess potential solutions to the issue. She couldn't hear the suggestions we made and as she led us through a maze of boxes. We quickly realized why the cats had become upset. Cardboard boxes and random items filled the home from floor to ceiling. As we followed the frazzled woman through her self-created maze, the piles grew before our eyes. When we finally reached her bedroom, she pointed to the cats as if they were nothing more than filthy garbage. The cats weren't in her bedroom. They were outside of the window – on the ground in the cold. "There. They have to live there because they only want to hurt me." Sitting beneath the piles were two adult cats crammed into what looked like an old birdcage. The cats were unable to stand and the cage consisted only of a litter box, no food or water bowls. Their sad eyes rose upwards to meet ours as we stared back at them, shocked at their tight living quarters. We knew at that moment the only hope for the cats survival would be being removed from the current environment. We agreed to take the cats into our organization that evening and scrambled to search for a foster home while we had them fully vetted and assessed.

We were able to keep the two cats together in their foster home and neither ever had an issue with the litter-box. You couldn't have asked for sweeter cats and it was clear that they were grateful for the reprieve they had been given. One cat was solid gray, the other solid black- both females. We named them Minnie and Mouse. Minnie the black cat was having a difficult time adjusting. Although she purred and loved being petted, she was depressed from losing the only home she had ever known. We worked with her daily to provide extra love and care and ensured she was receiving adequate nutrition. After a month of care, Minnie passed away in our arms and we attributed her death to a broken heart. Mouse pulled through the transition period and in time, she was adopted to a forever home to call her own; a home where she would never again be forced to live in a cramped cage. She was given the life that all pets deserve, a life of love and happiness.

We've taken in elderly owner surrender pets for various reasons throughout the years; a frail cat named Lady was surrendered to us when her guardian no longer wanted to care for her. And a thin gray senior cat named Bart came to us for nearly the same reason. Both Lady and Bart died within a week of being surrendered and it was clear their deaths came from broken hearts. They missed their guardians and longed for the bond they once shared, unable to understand why they would be tossed aside for nothing more than old age.

An elderly gray and white senior cat named Wanda came to us in much the same way. She was terribly thin and was left to fend for herself. It was my dog Lady who led me to Wanda. As she sat on the front porch of my work place, Wanda contemplated what to do next. Realizing Wanda's senior status and feeble condition, we committed to keeping Wanda within our organization for the duration of her life. This ensured she received the ongoing medical care and assistance she needed. Wanda gained weight and held her tail high as she trotted around greeting one person after the next. When she passed several months later, as her body was failing she fought to climb up to where we sat and pressed herself between two of us. Placing her paw in my hand, she fell asleep and passed away as quietly as she entered our lives. The moral of the story? I'm not sure there is one other than to know that relinquishing a pet is incredibly tough on the pet. Pet's suffer from broken hearts; often it takes a significant toll on their health – a toll often unseen or known by the owners who are so quick to give away their pets.

As a rescue organization, you will decide how to assess each situation that is presented to you and how to best proceed.

Charlie's Story

As I was standing on the porch talking to my mailman

one recent afternoon, he pointed out a cat was perched on the top corner of our privacy fence. I glanced behind me and sure enough there was a solid gray adult cat staring back at us, as if to say **"yes, I'm here and I'm hungry."** The moment the mail carrier turned to head back to his truck and left on his way, I trotted over to the fence to greet the stray feline. He quickly hopped down into the wispy grass of the yard next to ours and lay down as if he had been there all along. Making myself small, I crouched down to my knees and spoke softly to him, hoping to coax him towards me.

I knelt about a foot away from where he lay and I could tell that his hair- what he had left of it- was incredibly thin. He had countless scars from his tail to his head; his ears were nicked in multiple places from previous injuries. Chunks of hair were missing throughout his gaunt body. He had tall legs and a long body- he should have been a large cat- but instead he was merely a skeleton. His eyes sunk deep into his face and I could see the green mucus that had formed in the corner of his eyes. He needed medical attention. He needed nutrition. He needed water. I inched forward hoping I had gained his trust, but to no avail. He stood up and sprinted in the opposite direction into a fenced yard with two lively dogs. I ran the opposite way hoping he would come back towards me, away from the dogs. Quickly going inside to retrieve some canned cat food- I placed it in the stray bowl on the side of our home, hoping he would come back to find a good meal.

I didn't know if I would ever see him again, but low and behold, later that evening as I walked through the kitchen and happened to glance out the glass door that led to our backyard, there he was- walking on top of the perimeter of the fence. He walked carefully, slowly looking into our yard, hoping to find a meal; hoping, I thought, to find a few moments of peace and safety from his difficult life.

I watched, holding my breath as the thin gray cat hopped into our backyard and headed up to the deck. A few moments later I walked out carefully – so I would not spook him. With two bowls of food in hand, I crouched down and slowly approached him. He let me sit next to him as he devoured the food and drank a full bowl of water. I wanted to grab him, to bring him indoors and take care of him- but I knew I still had to earn his trust. I didn't want him to flip out in fear when I carried him to safety indoors. I wanted him to know he was safe; I was here to help in whatever way he needed. He was clearly in need.

The next day I came home to find several food bowls

placed throughout our yard. I wondered if someone else was trying to catch the stray cat. I looked around and as if he were waiting for me to arrive, there he was, laying softly in the grass on the side of our house- basking in the sunlight. I walked softly towards him, hoping he would recognize me. He did. Within moments I held him in my arms and took him indoors to safety. The neighbors watched me hold him and came out to ask if he would be okay. They worried about him too. I learned they had placed the bowls around the yard, hoping to provide him with a meal. Hoping he would survive. I let them know I was making a veterinary appointment and for tonight he would stay in a spare room in our house—we immediately treated him for ear mites, fleas, worms and parasites- all of which he undoubtedly had. I gave him a large bowl of water, a large bowl of dry food and a plate of moist canned cat food—a buffet to welcome him to safety. He was slow-moving and I suspected he was elderly, but upon closer inspection, we found he was a young adult cat- estimated to be 4-5 years old. It was clear he had been out on his own for years, trying to survive the best he knew how.

How he found us in his final days, I have no idea- but I am glad he did.

We named him Charlie– it just seemed to fit. You

could not just feel every bone in his body- you could see the outlines of each and every brittle bone. He was terribly dehydrated and emaciated. He was weak from years of running, years of being yelled at to get off someone's property, years of being kicked, years of hiding- simply trying to survive. Although in my heart of hearts, I hoped that Charlie would survive- and having been in animal rescue/rehabilitation for more than a decade of my life- I knew miracles could and sometimes did happen- my heart told me Charlie had found us too late. I hoped, and we did everything we could for him, but hope was not enough. Within 24 hours, Charlie passed away in his private room we had quickly welcomed him into; he had plush blankets and fluffy pillows. He had safety- possibly for the first time in years (maybe, ever). And Charlie, maybe for the first time, had love.

After Charlie ate and drank upon his arrival, he plopped down, as if onto a cloud, on a fluffy blanket we had placed out for him. He placed his head near the cool breeze of the air conditioning vent- feeling the movement hit his face as he no longer had to worry about the harsh impact of the burning rays of sunlight he could never before seem to escape. I pet Charlie from head to toe, I rubbed behind his ears, and I sat with him- knowing he was transitioning, and wanting him to know he could do so here, in peace- and with love.

Charlie passed away of kidney failure- which can happen when a feline has gone too long with starvation and dehydration. I wished more than anything he could have survived, that he could have stayed with us more than 24 hours- that he could have known what it was like to live the pampered indoor life, surrounded by love and laughter, to always have food, water and shelter and never again worry about safety. But it seemed Charlie had found us to transition into the afterlife in peace and surrounded by love.

We always keep an eye on stray cats in the area- as we want to make sure they are all spayed/neutered and they always have access to food, water and shelter. Charlie was new, no one in the neighborhood had seen him before. We don't know Charlie's background or where he came from, we don't know how or why he found us- but it was clear he had sought out our home. He had, it seemed, specifically sought out me. I don't know how he knew I was the person to find, but somehow he did and I'm thankful for that. I'm thankful he found me and was able to pass in peace and surrounded by love. I'm thankful he had good food and fresh water before he left this Earth. I'm thankful he knew what it was like to be held and petted, to be safe. Of course I wish he could have stayed with us much longer- I wish we could have saved him, but then I remind myself that maybe we did save him after all. Maybe we did save him from dying alone, from dying on the street and leaving the world wondering if love was merely a myth. Maybe we helped him in the best way we possibly could- we gave him what he came for; a peaceful, safe place to rest in peace.

I didn't know Charlie very long, but he has left a lasting impression on my heart. I've rescued and rehabilitated animals in need since the time I could walk and I feel that every life is truly precious- but there are certainly ones that leave a deeper imprint on your heart- and Charlie was one of those souls. Charlie taught me that finding peace, love and safety at any point in your life is important and we all need those elements in our own journeys. It's never too late to love, it's never too late to be embraced with kindness...And as Charlie showed me, it's never too late to find what you're looking for: even if what you're looking for happens to be a safe haven to rest in peace.

(Shared from the Advocates 4 Animals- Paw Prints Blog; 2013)

CHAPTER 11 CHALLENGE

- How will you respond to pleas for help for owned animals with known behavior issues?

- Will you provide a return clause in your adoption contract?

- What resources will you provide to those wanting to return a pet to your organization?

- What will be your protocol for a return request?

- Will your organization offer behavior training for adopters? How will this program work?

- Will your organization work/hire a professional dog (pet) trainer?

- Have you studied animal behavior? Are you aware of environmental issues that may cause behavior issues in pets? How will you inquire about potential issues with adopters wishing to return a pet? How will you assess what is in the best interest of the individual pet in question? Take time to speak with and learn from pet trainers and behaviorists. Learn how specific unwanted pet behaviors can be easily corrected. Your knowledge on this topic can help pets stay in their homes, rather than being needlessly relinquished to shelters or rescues.

12

COMING TOGETHER

———————

PERHAPS THE BEATLES SANG it best in their song *"Come Together"*. The two-word phrase is repeated a dozen times throughout the song. Okay, so the Beatles weren't talking about collaborations between shelters and rescues. There are a number of theories proposed for the meaning of the song. But I digress. The phrase alone speaks volumes. *Come Together*. No matter the endeavor, doesn't coming together typically yield better results?

Not only is it imperative you come together with

your local community, but it is equally as essential to helping the animals, that you collaborate with your local pound/shelter facility and with surrounding 501(c)3 rescue organizations.

Sound easy? Sadly, that's typically untrue. As with any business decision, there are a lot of considerations to review prior to jumping in. Previously, we mentioned the mistake many rescue organizations make is to march into their local pound without a plan and quickly announce they are there to save the animals. While it would certainly be empowering to put on our capes and fly into every shelter from California to New York and claim we could save every animal's life, the reality is we are one person- perhaps a small group of individuals -and we can make a difference, but we need to start locally and we need to embrace a tactical and judicious plan if we strive to make a true and lasting impact for the animals.

It may surprise you to learn that many open intake shelters do not wish to work with rescue organizations at all. It's mind boggling, but many open intake facilities are stuck in their traditional ways; utilizing killing as the only means to an end. They're not taking a moment to pause and realize that what they've done for centuries (i.e. killing innocent pets) isn't working. It isn't helping the animals and it isn't helping the tax-payers wallets.

Our own county pound's most recent annual statistics show that they saved a mere 18% of what they deemed healthy, sociable, friendly felines. They killed 100% of shy, feral, ill or injured felines. They do not have a volunteer foster program, they do not do adoption events, they are less than welcoming when you visit the facility as a potential adopter, they do not believe in TNR (trap/neuter/release for feral cats) and they do not invite volunteers from the community to come in and walk the dogs or play with the cats to provide daily attention. They are a facility that takes in animals and for the few that they agree to give a short run at adoption, they let them sit alone behind the bars of a lonely cage and wait. The shelter is hidden in an industrial area and there are no clear signs directing you to "Adopt A Pet Today!" There are no balloons or friendly attributes at all. Just a stark concrete building which houses needless daily killing rituals and a select few "adoptable" animals housed in cages – pets that may or may not be adopted. Just because they're on the adoption floor today doesn't mean they won't be next in line for "euthanasia" tomorrow.

It's taken us nearly 11 years of calling, visiting, and pleading to work with this particular pound. Every time we made contact with the pound, asking to help, they told us "no". They fed us the following lines each time we made a new attempt to collaborate:

- "There are no rescues in our county" [Every time we would reply telling them WE are a 501(c)3 rescue- but again they would say there are not any here]

- "We do the best we can. We don't need help with kittens. We work with rescues." [This, obviously was a blatant lie. They had never contracted with a rescue and we were a rescue calling to work with them].

- "Sure, we'll call you if we have anyone that we'll be putting down." [We never received a call. Not once. Yet the shelter director himself has admitted to killing lives 365 days a year].

- "You can foster for us. We'll tell you when their time is up." [We didn't want to foster *for* them-we wanted to get the animals out of that facility where they were facing certain death. We have our own adoption program and want to foster and adopt through our program. We certainly did not want to foster for them and receive a call a week later from them telling us that they were taking the kittens/cats back to euthanize them simply because they had the power to do so].

- "We don't need help with kittens. We do really well with cats. We have a high adoption rate." [Really? An 18% save rate of cats deemed healthy and adoptable by arbitrary standards is a high adoption rate?]

The list of bogus replies could fill a book of their own. It would be kind to say we were given the run around. We had countless volunteers call asking to foster *for* the shelter, asking to come in and walk the dogs- all requests were denied.

How do you establish a collaboration with an open intake shelter under power-hungry leadership and a view that daily killing is totally appropriate? How do you begin to communicate with a shelter whose leader and employees believe that an 18% save rate is applaudable?

Persistence.

While working on another community project, years later we were lead to communications with the new City Manager *by pure chance*. Inevitably via our communications, we mentioned our goal of working with the county pound to change the reality of pets who were unfortunate enough to find themselves there. The City Manager agreed and we struck up a conversation that wound up assisting us in getting our foot in the door of the very county pound we had worked 11 years to collaborate with. We followed through by submitting a formal proposal to the pound's director which lead to a sit-down meeting with the director and the pound's staff. When you're working with an open intake shelter that embraces killing, you walk a thin line when it comes to communicating. While it would have been easy to put on our Superman capes and feel like heroes for a day, we found ourselves sticking directly to the plan we had formally proposed with blessings from the City Manager. There were moments we would have loved to roll our eyes and state the obvious;

for example, when the pound director attempted yet another choke hold on us- a desperate attempt for control- telling us that *he* didn't believe in the way we ran *our* programs. We wanted to stand up and tell him that *we* didn't believe in *their* programs. But we bit our tongues. In situations like this, if the director sees you as a threat, he will simply cut off your access. One wrong step and poof- just like *that* our soon-to-be collaboration (the first collaboration ever established by a 501(c)3 No Kill organization with this pound) would be nixed.

Sadly, too often it is about a power trip for the directors and employees of open-intake shelters who believe that killing is appropriate. For us, it's not about power or control- it's simply about the animals. How can we work together to save more lives? How can we work together to increase awareness and adoptions in our local community? It's never been a competition for us; for us it has always been about doing what's right.

Collaborating with open intake shelters/pounds

Every open intake shelter will yield a brand new

experience. Throughout the first decade of operating Advocates 4 Animals, we worked with open intake shelters throughout Ohio, Indiana and Kentucky. We consulted shelters outside of those states as well when guidance was requested. We worked with one shelter at a time, helping to establish a system that allowed the shelter to form collaborations with 501(c)3 No Kill rescue organizations far and wide. We assisted in arranging trusted transport systems and encouraging volunteer photographers to visit their shelters in an attempt to spread the word about pets in need. We helped form standards and protocols for rescues to become approved partners with each particular shelter. We assisted shelters with "how to" steps as they worked to join Facebook or other social media resources for the first time, gaining additional exposure for their adoptable pets. We worked with the shelters who said yes to collaborating, in hopes of gaining more adoptions and lessening needless euthanasia. We worked with the shelters whose volunteers came to us for guidance and support.

All the while we hoped to begin collaborating with our local county pound, the one with the dismal 18% feline save rate; and all the while they ignored our requests to assist. So we helped the shelters who *were* willing to work together on behalf of the animals. Our collaborative experiences working with shelters throughout the Midwest proved to be both an educational and inspirational experience. It wasn't because of us –Advocates 4 Animals- that the shelters we worked with became No Kill facilities, it was because they themselves had decided to work towards this worthy goal; it was because those very shelters sought out the assistance they needed to fulfill *their* vision.

Open Intake Facilities Currently Working with Rescues

Fortunately more open intake shelters/pounds are beginning to realize the benefits of working collaboratively with local approved 501(c)3 rescues. Shelters that have established protocols for working with rescues will already have a system in place. If you wish to work with a shelter that falls within this category, it is your job to reach out to the shelter and follow their steps and guidelines to become an approved rescue. Often these shelters will have their rescue guidelines outlined on their website.

Prior to completing the shelter's approval process, you may want to research or ask questions in regard to this facility. Listed below are a few starter questions:

- How many rescue groups do you currently work with?

- Do the groups you work with typically pull cats *or* dogs?

- Where is your biggest need for assistance (i.e. senior dogs, orphaned kittens, et cetera)

- What is your pull fee? (**a pull fee is the fee charged by the shelter to a rescue, for each pet saved*)

- Will you call or e-mail us each week with pets in need or do we need to physically come in to the shelter once a week to view the pets?

When open intake shelters and approved rescue organizations work together, amazing feats are accomplished –pets are adopted and lives are saved. Successful collaborative efforts realize that it's not about wrestling for power or control; it's about doing what we've vowed to do; save lives.

Open Intake Facilities Who Have Never Worked with Rescues

Approaching an open intake facility that has previously never collaborated with a rescue organization can present a challenge. Do they wish to increase their adoption rates? Do they wish to lower their euthanasia statistics?

Presenting a well thought-out plan to the shelter director is often a good starting point. How can you help the shelter? It is a good idea to share references with the shelter director from other shelters you have worked with.

Does the shelter director feel that their biggest need is for assistance with orphaned kittens (those needing bottle fed around the clock)? Find out where they feel their biggest need is and why. Can your organization assist in that area? If so, explain to the director exactly how you can provide assistance in their area of need and be sure to provide an approximate number of pets you will be able to pull each week, month or year. Share your past annual adoption statistics with the director to show your success rate in locating forever homes.

Once the shelter director has agreed to work with your organization (allowing you to pull those pets they would otherwise euthanize), you may want to ask several questions as you embark on your new relationship:

- What is pull fee for each pet we save? What vetting is done (if any) prior to our group pulling the pet?

- Do you require that we provide proof of the pets spay/neuter with our organizations veterinarian?

- Will you call or e-mail us to let us know when you have pets who our group can pull or do we need to establish a day each week where we come to view the pets in need?

- Are you open to working with additional rescue

organizations? If so, we would be happy to refer other rescues to contact you to begin collaborating to assist additional pets at your facility.

After beginning work with our local county pound- to pull death row cats in need – one of our volunteers stopped by the shelter to pick up several cats we were saving. As she loaded up the lucky felines that we had secured volunteer foster homes for, she noticed a feral (or possibly very scared) cat with her newborn kittens hunkered down in the back of their steel cage. They had been placed in the line of cages awaiting the deadly injection. Our volunteer generously offered to take the mom cat and her babies- along with the crew we had already agreed to save that day. The director swiftly said no. When our volunteer asked why, the shelter director said the mom cat was feral and "needed" to be euthanized. He said the newborn babies would be needing rescue next week when the mom was gone and he would call us to take in and bottle-feed her babies. Our volunteer kindly persisted, asking to take in the mom cat and reminding the director we have resources for feral cats and once the babies were fully weaned we would have the mom spayed and vetted. If she turned out to truly be feral, she could be released in one of our managed feral colonies and have a good life. The director continued shaking his head and saying no- it wasn't going to happen. Again, it was about power and control. He wanted to make known to our volunteer she was not going to call the shots. She offered to pay an extra pull fee- in addition to what we already paid for each cat we saved from the shelter. Still, he said no. He refused to give in. Our volunteer left with 6 lucky cats in tow, but feeling defeated to know the feral (or possibly scared) mom cat would be dead in a matter of hours through no fault of her own. She arrived teary eyed and upset, telling us she tried everything she could to save the mom. Several days later we received a call that the shelter needed us to take in a litter of newborn kittens who had "lost" their mom. We knew exactly who they were referring to and it broke our hearts. This, from a shelter we had just recently forged a collaborative relationship with to save cats.

While it can be an uphill battle to embark on

a relationship with an open intake shelter whose director believes that killing is both necessary and appropriate – it is possible, but the struggles never seem to end. We continue our work with the local pound, pulling death row cats whenever possible- but ultimately our hope is for a compassionate director to take over. In our city we realize this may be nothing more than a pipe dream, but we continue to do everything we can through our multitude of programs to keep animals from ever entering the shelter. We continue to work to pull pets from their barred cages as often as we are able. We are one organization working to make a difference with a focus on local lives in need. But we realize that until a compassionate, motivated leader is hired at the pound– we are limited as to how many lives we can save. A shelter director must embrace the No Kill Equation; they must *want* to create a better life for the animals in their care if an indelible difference is going to be made.

Joining forces with other area 501(c)3 No Kill rescue organizations

As you establish collaborations with your local

open intake shelters you will realize that inviting additional approved rescue organizations to pull pets in need from the same shelter(s) will serve to save additional lives. Reach out to other 501(c)3 rescue groups in your area- are they willing to take in one shelter pet if you drive the pet to them? Often if you ask each area rescue to take in one pet, there is a high possibility they will make room and agree. Once you have established a strong relationship with a shelter in need in your area, reach out to other rescue groups and ask if they would be interested in doing the same. If you are able to provide assistance with transporting the pet from the shelter to their rescue, the group may be more likely to take in a pet in need.

Not all rescues want to work with shelters. Some rescues focus solely on owner surrender pets, while others keep their focus on stray pets or feral cats. Every rescue has its niche and sometimes learning exactly what their specialty is can assist you in working with them to save one more life from shelter death. If you find a local group that specializes in helping special needs dogs weighing less than 10 pounds, ask if they would be willing to take in dogs that fit this description when/if you come across them at the shelter you are working with.

You will ultimately discover your own path as you move forward in working with open intake shelters and other limited intake rescues. Although some rescue organizations see themselves as "competitors" with other rescue groups, the reality is we are all in this together whether you like it or not. If your organization is truly focused on the goal of making a difference in the lives of animals in need, competition will be the furthest thing from your mind. Stay focused on what you do best- saving and adopting lives in need; that is where a truly positive impact is made.

CHAPTER 12 CHALLENGE

- Review your county pound's statistics. How many cats and dogs are they saving each year? Do they implement a TNR program for feral cats? Do they have behavior training programs available for their canine adopters?

- What 501(c)3 rescue organizations and/or shelters exist in your area? Do your research. How many organizations can you locate within a 60 mile radius? Are they open intake organizations or limited intake? Do they have facilities or are they foster-based? Are they No Kill organizations?

- Does your local open intake pound/shelter work with approved rescue organizations currently? If not, have you called to inquire as to why?

- If another local rescue organization is already actively working with your local open intake shelter, contact the rescue organization and schedule a time to meet. What has their experience been like with the shelter? How did they start working with the shelter? Is a formal proposal needed? What do they recommend your organization do in order to begin working to save additional lives at the same shelter?

13

WE LOVE WILD CATS

———

GO WILD CATS? There is often much debate in regard to issues surrounding feral cats. Traditionally animal control utilizes euthanasia as an attempt at population control for cats deemed feral. However, there is a more compassionate and humane way to assist feral and stray cats in need. Not only is killing unnecessary, killing doesn't decrease the numbers as often argued. The only proven long-term population control is active sterilization and colony management. When feral

———

and stray cats are spayed and neutered and have a colony caretaker to provide huts (shelter) and daily food and water, the cats can live quality lives and through attrition the population will naturally diminish over time.

Altered feral and stray cats are of great assistance to rodent control, so much so that many farmers, horse sanctuaries, neighborhoods and even some restaurant areas embrace the many benefits delivered by feral cats. The key is to spay and neuter every cat in the colony. Leaving one unaltered female will create many additional cats over the course of just one year.

A feral cat is a cat who is not socialized to live with people. Feral cats are fearful and generally avoid people. Feral cats live healthy lives on their own, content in their outdoor homes. *Alley Cat Allies*, a national non-profit organization based in Maryland offers valuable pamphlets, flyers, videos and articles with further information on assisting feral cats.

A stray cat is not the same as a feral cat. A stray cat is friendly to people and can generally be adopted. Stray cats are often previously owned cats who have been sadly left behind and placed out doors to fend for themselves.

How do you alter a feral cat that you cannot touch? Read on...

TNR stands for Trap, Neuter, Release. Add an "M" on the end for *Manage* and you have the healthy elements in place for assisting feral cats. Even if you're a dog rescue, it's still important to understand the basics of TNR(M) so that you can provide, at minimum, basic guidance on the process to those who will contact your organization in search of assistance. In addition, there are many dog rescues that have been called into action to assist a terrified stray dog in need and humane traps (albeit much larger traps) are used to successfully catch and work with the stray dog.

Humane Traps are purchased online at Amazon and other websites or are found in local stores like Tractor Supply Company. A standard size trap is generally effective for most cats. However, if you are working to catch small kittens, you may need to acquire a smaller trap (as the young kittens are not heavy enough to trigger the standard size trap). In special cases, you may need an extra-large trap to catch large or injured cats who cannot comfortably fit into a standard size trap.

When trapping a feral or stray cat to have them altered with your veterinarian, it is important to take away all other food sources on the evening you are trying to trap the cat(s). In addition, be certain to place the trap in a quiet area where the cat(s) generally comes to eat. It is important the ground is flat. In the back of the trap, place a bowl of canned cat food; be sure it is placed in the very back of the cage so that the cat entering the trap will successfully trigger the door. It is helpful to place a very small trail of the canned food just prior to the trap trigger to entice the cat to enter. When a trap is set, be sure to check the trap often-especially in extremely hot or cold temperatures.

Sometimes you are able to catch the cat(s) on your first attempt, however, if you are working to assist a larger colony, patience and persistence are key. Once the cat is caught take him/her to your veterinarian right away for spay/neuter surgery. For feral cats, ask the veterinarian to "tip" the cat's ear. Tipping a feral cat's ear is a universal sign indicating that this cat has been successfully altered. This makes it easier if you are working with a colony of multiple cats (so you know who has already been fixed). If the cat is a friendly stray you may not need to use a trap at all. However, if they are scared and uncertain, a trap may be helpful to assisting them. When a stray cat is spayed/neutered, if you plan to take him/her in and foster them until an adopter is found, an ear tip is not necessary. Many veterinarians are placing a small green tattoo on the cat's stomach to indicate the cat has been altered. This is incredibly helpful if the cat ever becomes lost in the future as other veterinarians and rescues will know that the cat has already been altered and does not need to undergo surgery for this purpose.

When working with feral cats or a feral cat colony, it is important to return the cats to the same location where you rescued them- unless they are in immediate danger. Feral cats have difficulty readjusting to new areas. However, if the situation warrants the relocation of feral cat(s) in order to survive (i.e. if those in the area where the feral cats were living are threatening to harm or kill the feral cats) it is imperative that specific steps are followed to assist with a successful transition.

Steps to successfully relocating feral cats:

IndyFeral, a non-profit organization located in Indiana, explains "Relocation is the process of moving a stray or feral cat from its current outdoor home to a new outdoor home. It is a labor intensive process and often times has a low success rate. Cats are very territorial and remaining in their current habitat is optimal for their health and safety." On occasion there are situations that do warrant relocation and Indy feral shares those situations as:

- The lives of the cats are being threatened in a way that cannot be legally remedied.

- The colony is located on public or private property that will not allow the maintenance of the colony.

- Their home or shelter is being destroyed and it is impossible to provide an alternative shelter at their current habitat or migration of the cats within a reasonable distance is not possible.

- There is no identifiable caretaker.

Colony cats develop strong bonds with each other and best thrive in their natural environments; for many, it is the only home they've ever known. If you can prevent the need for relocation, this is highly recommended. The cats are comfortable where they are living and can live healthy, happy lives when altered and when a colony caretaker is appointed.

Several concerns both Alley Cat Allies and Indy Feral point out in regard to relocating feral/stray cats:

- Cats may disappear once relocated. Often other cats in the area will be territorial and run the "new arrival cats" off from the area. In addition, cats have a natural instinct to return home and will often become lost or killed when they attempt this journey (i.e. hit by cars). In addition, because of the relationships cats form with other colony cats, when relocated cats will often miss the other colony members and suffer from depression and stress.

- A new environment can bring new threats that are unrecognizable to the relocated cats (i.e. the relocation of a city cat to a rural area, they now need to worry about farm equipment, coyotes, et cetera).

Beware of the "vacuum effect". Indy Feral shares, "Relocating all or most of the cats in a colony can open up a void called the vacuum effect. This allows unsterilized cats to move into the area, starting the cycle all over again if there is shelter or food to attract them. The food supply could be unsecured trash cans, an unknown feeder or wild rodents."

If you absolutely have to relocate a feral cat colony in order to keep them safe, please adhere to the following guidelines when doing so:

- Locate a "safe and permanent home site with a caretaker committed to providing life-long feeding, watering, medical care and monitoring of the cats." Finding a proper relocation site can be incredibly difficult.

- Items you will need to assist in the relocation

process: humane traps, large wire dog crates (Indy Feral recommends a minimum size of 2 ft x 3 ft), litter boxes and litter (for inside the cages), food and water bowls (in addition to food and water), blankets to cover the wire dog crates "to help reduce the cat's stress."

- "Identify a room or secure area that is clean, quiet, temperature controlled and protects cats from the elements as much as possible. Be sure there is adequate air and light available." This is the room where you will first bring the relocated cats (in the dog crates) to begin adjusting to their new environment.

- Keep one or two cats in each large dog crate (remember to place a blanket over the top and back areas of the wire dog crate, to create some privacy for the feral cats during their adjustment phase). Be sure to include the food, water and litter box in each crate. Confine the cats in their crates in the designated room/area and keep the cats near each other, allowing them to see and smell their new environment and caretaker.

- Keep the cats confined to their large wire dog crates for a minimum of 2-3 weeks as their relocation site. The colony caretaker will provide daily food, water and litter box cleaning during this time and the cats will begin to adjust to the caretaker as well as to the new environment during this time. The colony caretaker should speak softly to the cats and visit them a minimum of two times daily, each time bringing additional food and checking their water bowl levels. Feeding plenty of canned cat food is very helpful during this phase as many cats love the smell and taste and will begin to then associate the caretaker as positive. Provide dry food also. After the 2-3 week confinement phase, the caretaker should release the cats by opening their cage doors (understand that the cats will most likely run and hide). The caretaker should continue feeding twice a day at the same times he/she has been and in the same location. Following these steps will provide the best chance for success at relocation.

Establishing a Colony Caretaker:

How do you find a colony caretaker or better yet,

several caretakers? Every situation is different. Who called to report a need for assistance with the neighborhood feral cat colony? Are they willing to step up to provide daily food, water and shelter (huts)? It is best if you can find someone living in the area to appoint as the caretaker. If you can find a back-up or a second caretaker, that is even better (i.e. in case the colony caretaker is ill, out of town, et cetera).

If you are unable to locate an adequate colony caretaker who lives in the area, consider establishing Community Ambassadors as we do at Advocates 4 Animals. Appoint Community Ambassadors for each city or town in your area of service. Ambassadors are committed, experienced volunteers who are well-versed in caring for feral cat colonies. If you decide to utilize this method, we recommend an interview process prior to appointing a new Community Ambassador; also new Ambassador can shadow a veteran Ambassador to learn the ropes of becoming a designated Colony Caretaker for feral cat colonies in that Ambassador's area.

Purchasing or building shelter (huts) for feral and stray cats:

There are countless options when it comes to providing adequate shelter (huts) for feral and stray cats. You can build your own, use a pre-owned dog hut or purchase anything from a simple insulated hut to a deluxe hut that can be well-hidden in your yard.

Lining the huts with Mylar blankets and straw will help the cats stay warm during inclement weather. In addition, consider attaching a flap once the cat(s) has warmed up to the hut- to keep cats out of the wind (and blowing snow/rain/ice).

Placing the hut(s) near the food source is important to allow cats to locate the shelter.

Specific DIY instructions on feral cat huts are found in the following places:

- CAT FANCY Magazine (December 2014 edition)
- Alley Cat Allies website
- Indy Feral website

- Advocates 4 Animals website

- You can also search on YouTube for "How To" videos and visual step-by-step instructions.

Five years ago we began working on a TNR/Feral cat project assisting an elderly lady who was overwhelmed by feral cats. Having lived in her home for more than fifty-years, Patty's street was now filled with vacant homes often running rampant with crime. After surviving several traumas of her own, Patty found solace in feeding the stray cats in her area and longed to help. When Patty contacted Advocates 4 Animals, close to one-hundred stray and feral cats were roaming her street and hoping for assistance. Our pet food pantry provides Patty with regular food and our spay/neuter program has been working with Patty's colony for more than five years to spay and neuter every cat in need. Inevitably some of the cats are friendly and are placed into our rescue/ adoption program and ultimately find forever homes to call their own. The feral cats are altered and returned while Patty continues to provide daily food and water. We have trained Patty to successfully utilize a humane trap so when new cats arrive to the colony she can work on trapping him/her immediately. We have assisted in building multiple straw lined huts for Patty's feral cats as well. To date, we have altered every cat in the colony, however, recently two additional cats have showed up. *Both females.* As with many TNR projects this is ongoing and may always be. But in keeping in regular contact with the colony caretaker we are able to ensure that a large colony of feral cats are altered, have regular food and water and are adequately prepared to live outdoors.

As they so often do, another feral cat project we were working on turned into a much larger project than initially expected. We were told six cats at an apartment complex were in need. No one could touch them and the apartment manager wanted them gone. Local residents had been known to shoot at the cats and torment them. The project took us close to four years and over that time more than 70 cats were saved. In this particular project it was necessary to relocate the cats and we did so utilizing multiple barn homes in our program that offered to provide everything the cats needed both to transition and to live happy outdoor lives on the farm.

Generally, we have multiple TNR projects occurring throughout our local area at any given time in addition to the long-term projects which we keep in contact with and help to manage. Whether it's a neighborhood, a fairgrounds or a busy downtown area, all feral and stray cats are in desperate need of assistance. If your organization does not choose to implement a TNR program, be sure to locate local agencies that do so that you can provide proper referrals to those in need when inquiries arise. A successful TNR program will include:

- Humane trapping assistance – *including the rental of traps*

- Spay/Neuter assistance – *possibly assistance with transporting as well*

- Cat food assistance

- Guidance as to how to build or where to purchase affordable cat huts/shelters

- Assistance in locating a local colony caretaker to provide daily food/water for the cats

Every feral cat project is different. Whether there are one or one-hundred cats in need, your organization can make a huge difference through providing education and assistance with TNR and possibly with a food donation (if needed) to an established colony caretaker.

Assisting stray and feral cats helps to save thousands of lives from shelter death every year. Alley Cat Allies reports that more than 70% of cats who enter shelters in the United States are euthanized; nearly 100% of shy and feral cats are killed. Shelter euthanasia is the leading cause of death (greater than any disease) for cats. In addition, by altering just one cat, you are preventing countless litters of future kittens. Implementing a TNR program in your organization is an incredible gift to your community and to the feral and stray cats who live there and are waiting for your help.

CHAPTER 13 CHALLENGE:

- Will your organization specialize in TNR(M)? Or will you refer those needing assistance with feral cats to other local organizations? If you plan on referring these inquiries to others, what 501(c)3 organizations in your county provide TNR training and assistance?

- Does your local county pound utilize TNR or do they merely euthanize feral cats upon intake? If they are not currently employing TNR methods, speak with them to ask about doing so. Will they allow a volunteer to provide monthly TNR classes and teach the local public how to become colony caretakers for feral cats?

- If your organization plans on implementing a TNR program, what will you do with feral cats who need relocation? Do you have several barn homes that are willing to work with you once the cats are altered?

14

GET YOUR MEDIA MOJO ON

———————

NON-PROFIT IS TYPICALLY synonymous with limited funding. So how do you gain quality media exposure when you're on a limited budget? Just like everything else in life...hard work and endless persistence!

Thinking outside of the proverbial box is a no-brainer here. If you want people to know about the work you're doing and how you're helping the local community, start spreading the word. The first step though is to DO THE WORK YOU SAY YOU DO. Too many times well-intentioned individuals form organizations only to realize they don't really want to do the work that's required. Honesty and professionalism are essential to your credibility and longevity as an organization. An anonymous former volunteer for a rescue organization shared that the organization brought in more than $100K annually but only saved and adopted four animals a year. Not four-hundred. Four. They didn't operate any additional programs other than the rescue/adoption program- so where was the money going? Still other programs will "piggy-back" impactful organizations, closely mirroring their name and reaping the benefits of the confusion they've caused (all while not working to help the animals that donors believe *they* are helping).

It goes without saying that in today's modern world having a website for your organization is a must. The front page of your website should clearly state your organization's mission statement, contact information and the specific area you serve. In addition, it is beneficial to choose several social media outlets for your organization. You don't have to use every social media form available; instead choose one or a few social media outlets you enjoy and gain supporters and followers from those sources. When you narrow your focus on a few social media sources rather than spreading yourself thin trying to utilize every source available, you will build a loyal base of followers who look forward to reading about what project you'll be working on next.

It's important to do what you can with what you have; and focus on the positives. Don't just talk the talk...walk the walk! You've heard the expression before and it bears repeating, do the work that you say you do. Share your rescue and adoption stories via word of mouth and on your website and social media pages. Hold fundraisers and let people know what your organization is doing to help your local community and how they can support your work and get involved.

I published an article for *The Examiner* several years ago warning donors to be careful of where they donate their hard earned dollars (see below). Donors have a right to know how their dollars are being utilized. Before you begin your fundraising efforts, make a plan as to how much money you will need to raise for each animal rescued. How will you cover additional expenses that may arise? If donors donate towards a specific rescue project, how will you keep them updated on the progress of that endeavor?

DONATE LOCAL: UNDERSTANDING HOW YOUR DONATIONS ARE UTILIZED

When you donate to a 501c3 charity of your choice, do you know where your money is going? Do you donate to big name national charities like the Humane Society of the United States (HSUS), or do you choose to donate to local grassroots organizations giving back to your community? Who heads the organizations that you donate to? What are their motivations and aspirations for your local community and for the specific charity organization?

In 2010, the HSUS brought in $148,703,820.00 from donations alone. Many citizens and donors do not realize that the HSUS does not house any animals. They are not affiliated with any humane society organizations/shelters throughout the country that do house and adopt animals. They are simply a large independent organization collecting thousands in donations to advocate the unnecessary killing of animals in need of rescue and adoption. In 2009 alone, the HSUS spent over $8 million on direct mailing for solicitations and over $11 million in advertising expenses. The HSUS decided not to support Oreo's Law, a life-saving law for animals (New York). By not supporting Oreo's Law in New York, shelters have killed more than 25,000 animals. As both a legislative organization and a so-called progressive animal welfare organization, is it logical to withhold support for a law that saves animals? And to top it all off, the HSUS CEO/President, Wayne Pacelle was paid $234,026 in 2009 to do this work. In addition 15 staff members earned more than $100k each. Where did their salaries come from? You guessed it, public donations.

On a local level, let's take a look at Advocates 4 Animals Rescue & Rehabilitation, Inc.- a 501c3 grassroots rescue organization located in Xenia, OH. In 2010 A4A helped the local public to spay/neuter 315 pets. A4A rescued and adopted 105 animals locally- all rescued as local strays or from local high-kill shelters. A4A helped TNR (Trap/Neuter/Return) and care for 120 cat colonies locally. Did you know that an unspayed female cat, her mate and all of their surviving offspring, producing 2 litters per year, with only 2.8 surviving kittens per litter can total 66,088 cats in just 6 years? An unspayed female dog, her mate and all of their puppies can total 67,000 in 6 short years! By spaying/neutering and implementing TNR programs- A4A Rescue is saving thousands upon thousands of lives locally. A4A helped several local shelters begin their journey to becoming a true no-kill facility- through implementing the elements of the No Kill Equation (and through providing resources, volunteers and guidance throughout the process). A4A has no paid staff- they are all volunteers. A4A received a mere $22,000 in donations in 2010. Imagine how much more could locally be achieved if grassroots rescue organizations like A4A received the donations that are blindly mailed off to the HSUS annually. Just imagine how many more lives could actually be saved!

What are your motivations for donating? Whether it's animal rescue/welfare or any other worthy charitable cause, find out how your hard earned dollars will be used. Find out how many lives will be saved. How many staff and directors are being paid- and how much? Do you know the mission of the charitable organization and how they uphold those values? How do your donations help your local community?

By logging on to Guide Star you can search for your favorite 501c3 charities to find the donation total received the prior year. By visiting the websites, Facebook pages, Blog posts, fundraising events and by emailing or speaking with a volunteer from that organization you can gain a better sense of how donations are utilized. Mere statistics will get you started; contacting the organization(s) and its volunteers will give you a true sense of how your donations are assisting in charitable efforts. In a technology centered era the information is literally right at our fingertips: with only a few clicks, you can be sure your donations are supporting the issues you believe in. You have the power to decide whether your donations pad the wallets of CEO's like Wayne Pacelle of the HSUS, or whether your donations help make a true difference, a life-saving difference, at a local level- in your very own community.

CHAPTER 14 CHALLENGE

- Have you created a name for your organization? Have you purchased a website? Does your website include your organizations contact information, geographical coverage area (location) and your mission statement clearly on the front page?

- Are you utilizing social media?

- How many animals do you plan to rescue during your organization's first year? Do you have qualified foster homes established for this volume of intake? How many adoptions do you plan to complete in your first year? Do you have funding in place to cover veterinary bills and ongoing care for all of the animals you will rescue during your first year?

- Re-read your organizations mission statement.

Does the statement reflect the work you will be doing on a day-to-day basis?

15

DONATIONS PLEASE

WHETHER YOU ARE ESTABLISHING a non-profit to help animals, children, the environment, or anything in-between, it is essential to begin working on obtaining your 501c3 status. Your 501c3 status simply means your non-profit organization is exempt from federal income taxes for the activities designated by the organization. The status also allows donors to make federally tax deductible charitable contributions to your organization. In addition, most grant making opportunities require grantees to have their 501c3 exempt status prior to allowing any solicitation of funding.

There are many websites and legal firms that will help you step by step in filing your federally tax-exempt form 1023. Form 1023 is the IRS form that is reviewed and scrutinized to ensure your organization is a legitimate non-profit organization participating in charitable endeavors. Prior to completing your 1023, please review your organization mission and be sure to have your programs well thought out. It is beneficial to review form 1023 prior to completing the form so you are able to articulate the exact purpose of the organization.

Some of the most common reasons for denial are basic human errors – such as including the wrong filing fees, forgetting to include your EIN on each document prepared, and not completing all supplemental forms necessary. Form 1023 does require extensive paperwork, but please review, review and then review some more prior to submitting to the IRS. The typical wait time to receive your determination letter from the IRS is anywhere from 3 months to 12 months. If your paperwork has any errors, you are required to fix the errors and then re-submit (no extra money is paid to the IRS unless you submitted the incorrect filing fee) and then you start the waiting process over again. Like anything in life, it's best to do it right the first time.

The IRS submission will ask you to include information such as your Articles of Incorporation, your Board of Directors, narrative of activities, organization history, financial data – the list goes on and on. And you will ask yourself – what in the world did we get into? We just wanted to help animals (or kids or the environment). But as we have reiterated throughout the book – running a non-profit organization must be treated like a business. It's important to know your financials, have a strong Board of Directors who can enhance the quality of the organization and have your programs and activities well-defined. I will admit when we were going through the process of completing the 1023, there were days we just wanted to call it quits. The IRS required so much information. But we knew that in order to take our organization to the next level we had to obtain our tax-exempt status. In completing the

IRS form 1023, we learned quite a bit about our goals and objectives for the organization. We were no longer an organization who simply tried to help *every* animal in need, but we had become a non-profit business with specific goals and objectives that were realistic and focused and could really make an impact on our local community.

In forming your Board of Directors there are a number of things you may want to ask yourself before you start firing off emails and text messages to your friends and family asking them to join your Board of Directors. While it is most comfortable to surround yourself with those who are familiar, they may not always be the best choices for your Board of Directors. A successful organization is supported by a cohesive and well-rounded Board or Directors. Many Boards consist of 5-10 individuals who all have an important skill or trait that will be essential to your organization. It is also important to select Board members who share in your passion and commitment of your non-profit. While an affluent board member is great, if that affluence is not matched with passion for the mission of the non-profit, you are setting your

Board up to fail. When selecting Board members be sure to articulate your expectations of their role within the organization. Will your Board members be responsible for contributing a certain amount of finances to the organization annually? Will the Board members be responsible for organizing fundraisers and soliciting donors? Many animal welfare organizations solicit veterinarians to join their Board of directors. Other animal welfare organizations, depending on size, solicit attorneys, HR specialists, social media gurus and marketing geniuses to join their team. It is important to know your needs before you begin soliciting – you have to know where you are going if you are ever going to get there. And sometimes, in spite of all of your planning and best efforts, some boards just do not click – whether it is personality clashes or simply lackadaisical Board members. So it is important to establish realistic service terms (1 year as opposed to unlimited service terms). Like any relationship, sometimes it works and sometimes it doesn't. When it doesn't, it is important to go back to the drawing board and establish additional criteria to help create the Board of your dreams. Once you are satisfied with your Board and have formed a cohesive team, the sky is the limit.

As with everything in running an organization, nothing comes easy. Yes, you have spent hours compiling paperwork, figured out filing fees and waited and waited for your IRS determination letter stating you are officially a Federally Tax Exempt organization and you can now add to your website the 501c3 wording! So now the money starts pouring in – once donors find out your organization is a 501c3 – right? Unfortunately things don't work out that way. Yes, you can begin to apply for grants that you may not have been eligible to receive before the 501c3 approval and yes, you can add 501c3 after your non-profit name on anything and everything (letterhead, postcards, business cards, t-shirts, flyers, websites, social media) but please don't bank on thousands of dollars coming your way in the first few months.

Generally, your donors are earned over time and an official status from the IRS will not change that. In fact, our organization received its IRS approval letter in early 2009 and our revenues in 2009 were very similar to 2008. We did not receive a windfall of donors in 2009. In fact we have never had a windfall of donors. Our donors began supporting our organization very slowly and over time we have built a strong support team that helps us keep our organization in the black each year. We have donors who donate once and we never hear from them again, we have our annual donors, we have our donors who support us each month through our sponsorship programs and we have donors who are incredibly active and support our organization in nearly every endeavor. We treat each donor the same – with great appreciation and respect- because we know that over time $10 donations add up. If 1000 people donate just $10 suddenly you have raised $10,000 for your organization. We are incredibly grateful for every donor we have – regardless of the amount of money they donate. Although we have been operating since 2003 with our organization, I am still amazed each time we receive a donation. It's exciting to have others support the goal of helping to make the world a better place.

Fundraisers

Once you have received your approved determination letter from the IRS (and your dancing for joy ends!) the real work starts. Completing form 1023 was tough but it's nothing compared to balancing your budget, creating program budgets, establishing fundraisers and soliciting donors. Without money you don't go far in the world and in running a business whether for profit or non-profit, *cash is king*. It is important to establish a realistic budget. While it is easy to hope that you will receive a windfall of donations, realistically you will not. If one of your programs is to establish a low-cost spay and neuter program for the community, start small. In year one, you may only have the funding to offer 100 sterilization surgeries or you may only have the funds to rescue 50 pets in need. While that may not seem like much, **it is important to know your budget and stay within the parameters of that budget.** If you receive a call from a concerned citizen about 45 cats who are in need and your bank account is close to red-lining, it will be imperative to either solicit a collaborative effort with another organization or to refer to another organization with deeper pockets. It is very easy to get in over your head when you first start an organization, but finances will always tell you the truth. If your finances are low, it's time to start fundraising. Fundraisers are fantastic if they are well planned and well executed. Our organization has run the gamut of fundraising – from highly successful silent auction/dinners to events raising only $50 (on an all-day event). We have tried a multitude of methods. There are no guarantees when it comes to fundraising other than to take a risk and give something a calculated try. What works well for one organization may not bode well for another. There is not a "one size fits all" model.

Our annual Silent Auction/Dinner fundraiser takes approximately 9 months to plan and the week before the event, it seems like there are still hundreds of things to do. In the end, fundraising is about trial and error and taking risks and accepting that sometimes you will fail. But in each failure is a lesson on how to achieve success. The only magic formula we have in being a successful fundraising organization is to try many different fundraisers, cut the ones that don't work, tweak the ones that have the potential to be successful and carefully refine those that are successful so they can continue to grow become more successful each year. Ultimately you are on a journey to discover which events speak most to your supporters.

Grants

In addition to fundraisers, once you are an official 501c3 non-profit organization you can begin soliciting grant funding from foundations and other charities. Like anything, through trial and error, you will determine which grant makers and foundations respond favorably to your proposals. Our organization started out with absolutely no grant writing experience and we spent years reading, researching and trying to hone our grant proposals. Hundreds of query letters and full proposal submissions later, we continue to learn. While we certainly do not receive every grant we apply for, we do receive enough funding to run several successful programs within our organization. If there is anything to pass along to readers about grant writing, it is the two following words: *measurability and specificity*. Grant makers expect your proposals to be measurable and specific. Much like developing your mission, the focus of your grant proposal must be narrow. If you are writing a proposal for a spay and neuter program simply stating that you want funding for spay and neuter surgeries: will net you $0 in grant funding. But soliciting a grant maker with a proposal of obtaining funds for 100 spay and neuter surgeries for owned felines of low income residents below the poverty line in zip code 11111 during the months of June & July 2015 with results measurable by analyzing the number of intakes in the county shelter for zip code 11111 in 2015 vs. 2014 – that *may* earn your organization successful grant funding! That was a mouthful – but it's necessary for a quality proposal.

I remember the day we received our first large grant. We had been in operation for several years and operated on a shoe string budget day after day. We always had just enough to cover our veterinary bills and other expenses but we were uncertain of how to get to the next level. The foundation that provided the funding was extremely thorough. In fact, we have never to this day been as nervous as we were presenting to the foundation president that day. We succeeded in the interview process and were awarded the grant. But it was that grant that taught us exactly what was expected of our organization at the next level. Not only did we have the experience of learning from a foundation president, but the incredible boost of confidence we received was immeasurable. We were no longer a little organization on a shoe-string budget. We were a thriving, successful organization with community programs that were not only viable, but sustainable.

Executive Director

A successful organization starts with a good idea that is implemented. **A truly successful organization stays successful through great leadership.** The Executive Director position within an organization is the face of the organization. A good E.D. will operate a strong organization but a phenomenal E.D. will run a phenomenal organization. Have you ever gone into a store where you could just tell that the employee wanted to be anywhere *but* there? I bet if you asked to see the manager, they would exude much of the same energy. Attitude is contagious and a leader with a passionate, determined and committed attitude will run a stellar organization. Nathan Winograd, Director of The No Kill Advocacy Center often states that shelter reform must start with a compassionate leader. If the leader in a shelter rejects the notion of killing animals as a means of population control, then the staff will follow with the same attitude. At our local shelter, the director accepts killing as a means of population control and "euthanasia" is practiced on a daily basis per the shelter director's direction. Because he condones killing, the staff follows suit. Killing animals for space is *just part of the job* (the shelter used these words in speaking to us, explaining their position). To them, they see no other solutions. Again, attitude is contagious and if the leader believes killing for cage space is acceptable, then the staff follow suit. But if the leader truly embraced alternatives to convenience killing and showed through a passionate and determined attitude that there is no need to kill healthy, adoptable pets – the staff would follow suit with that as well. In turn, morale would increase and customer service and overall attitude of the shelter would increase. Animal's lives would be saved because of positive leadership.

Our organization believes in superior customer service. You may wonder how customer service plays a part in animal rescue – but it is the single most important tenet of our organization. We do little things that seem often overlooked by other organizations. We answer emails generally within 12 hours and always offer solutions and advice, even if we are not physically able to take a pet into our organization. All donors are treated the same – whether it's a $5 donation or a $500 donation, we believe in expressing our gratitude to every donor. $5 may be a huge amount of money to someone and we want them to know we value and appreciate their contribution. There are over 15,000 animal rescue organizations in the United States and we feel extremely grateful when anyone chooses to support our organization. Our goal is to make everyone who has contact with our organization-whether it is an adopter, a donor, or someone requesting help- feel positive about our organization and their experience. This type of customer service attitude is a direct result of our

Executive Director. It was the late Maya Angelou who said it best, *"People may not always remember the things you say to them, but they will always remember the way you make them feel."*

As co-founders of an organization/business, you rarely have time to think about how you got to where you are; how many little steps it took to get to the point you are at right now. For us, we knew we were concerned about the well-being of animals in our country's shelters and pounds. We spent years volunteering in shelters, working in kennels and at veterinary offices- researching the industry as a whole. We knew in our hearts that there was a better solution for homeless animals. It was a simple morning walk when our idea came to light – we should start an organization that helps animals called Advocates 4 Animals. And we did. We started a non-profit business that has completely changed our lives and the lives of so many others – both human and animal. The work is endless – whether it is balancing your revenue and expenses or saving 10 kittens from death row – it's all important to the sustainability of your organization. Loving animals is only the start of running a successful non-profit organization to help animals in need. We continue to learn that our passion ignites a fire within us but it's not enough to sustain a business long-term. Knowledge is power and the more knowledgeable we become, the more our businesses will excel.

CHAPTER 15 CHALLENGE

- Review animal welfare related grants [national, regional, and local grants] and learn the requirements for each.

- Review Form 1023 and begin gathering information necessary to complete 501c3 approval

- Begin to brainstorm for a potential Board of Directors: How will each member enhance your organization?

- Brainstorm possible fundraising ideas within your local community [Make a list of your ideas]

- Determine 5-10 potential fundraisers for your organization. Make a list. How will each specific fundraiser assist your organization? What will it take to host each fundraiser (cost, items needed, venue, etc.)? How much do you realistically expect to raise at each fundraiser? What time of year do you plan to hold each event? How will you find people to attend?

16

WHEN DO I GET A VACATION?

———————

WHEN DO YOU GET A VACATION? The truth is you don't. As a business owner you're responsible for every action of your organization and for the lives that you have rescued and promised to provide adequate and loving care to. If you're in search of a job that will provide you with limitless perks and vacations...*this is not it*. Prior to starting an animal rescue organization, it's important to realize that Compassion Fatigue is real and sadly runs rampant throughout many organizations. Everyone is at risk for Compassion Fatigue, especially those who are providing daily care to others.

Common symptoms of Compassion Fatigue include but are not limited to normal displays of chronic stress which result from the care giving work we provide. Be aware of the symptoms so you can develop a plan of action for when these moments occur.

An informative PetFinder.com article by Nancy Mullins shares, *"Research is starting to document that Animal Care Professionals are being traumatized in many of the same ways that other rescuers/first responders (firefighters, police, paramedics, corpsmen, service people in combat, Red Cross volunteers) are traumatized by what they witness. Some studies are beginning to suggest that animal care professionals may be #1 in vulnerability to Compassion Fatigue and Burnout."*

Mullins explains that the causes of Compassion Fatigue and Burnout are caused by a number of factors, including:

Constant exposure to trauma (i.e. horrific

rescues, animals who are dumped and/or who have been severely neglected or abused, et cetera).

"You are often dealing with at best an ignorant public, but often with an ungrateful or hostile public, or a finger-pointing public." Mullins continues, "Your jobs demand that you be courteous and try to educate, while inside you may be feeling despair about what's happening to animals in our country. You may feel angry or sick inside. Often you face a public that doesn't want to know what happens in shelters or out on the road in the truck. In our country, the realities of shelter work have been isolated. Coming out publically is important. We need to know."

Your work often carries over into your personal life

You are trying to do something to help with very limited resources or funding

Daily repetitive exposure to trauma and facing these trauma's alone, unable to take the time to talk about how you are feeling with someone who understands. Keeping your feelings held inside can hurt.

Can you avoid Compassion Fatigue? In a word, no. If you operate an animal rescue (or any daily care providing organization- for animals or humans) and expect to do so for the long haul, you are susceptible to Compassion Fatigue. It can strike at any time. You can be in the middle of a busy adoption season or simply doing your day-to-day rescue and rehabilitation work and bam, just like that Compassion Fatigue can knock the wind out of you. If you haven't experienced it for yourself, this may sound strange. Unfortunately Compassion Fatigue is an all too common reality for those in the animal rescue field. It can impact anyone from part-time volunteers to full-time employees. It can impact young and old, shelters and rescues. The harsh reality is that in a profession where you deal with trauma every day and in a profession where you have little to no time to talk about your grief with others, Compassion Fatigue may be inevitable.

As mentioned earlier in the book, when we first started Advocates 4 Animals we said "yes" to every inquiry we received...and there were a lot! A lot of pleas for help equaled a lot of yes's which equated to a high volume of intakes and of course limited funds and resources and limited foster homes that we could depend on. You have to find your focus and know your limits. At Advocates 4 Animals, each of us (co-founders) have work-a-holic tendencies and that, coupled with wanting to make a difference for lives in need in our community and knowing that there were no other viable resources or alternatives available...well, let's just say it was mind-blowing. The need for assistance with pets- and specifically cats- was and is astronomical. The countless daily pleas for help from the public alone left us feeling numb. Pet guardians wanting to relinquish their pets simply because they "didn't have enough time to spend with them", pets who had been sadly left behind when their guardians moved away- often times those very pets were unaltered and producing litter after litter. People found stray animals left and right and the unfathomable number of abuse and neglect cases we were called to assist on left our minds spinning night after night. We brought on foster homes only to find that many would "drop out" after a week or a month- leaving us in limbo with the pets we thought we had secured temporary placement for while we worked to find well-matched forever homes.

When we finally realized that we sometimes had

to "just say no" we were sure to provide viable resources to those individuals asking for assistance, hoping that another organization would step up to help. Often we received hateful e-mails in response to our suggestions. When people want us to take in their pets (and almost always it is "Urgent" or "No later than tonight...or else") they often become angry when we didn't rush to scene and take their pet into our custody immediately. It's a tough reality, but what's tough is that we worry about those very animals. We realize that as an organization we can do a lot, but we can't do everything alone. We have to set limits for our organization and for each of our volunteers and foster homes so that we avoid the onset of Compassion Fatigue as best as we can. We also have to set limits to make sure we always have adequate funding and resources to properly care for the animals already in our organization – to be sure that they have the best lives possible with us and once adopted. Quality care is non-negotiable.

We were called to action at a local horse track that was running rampant with unaltered stray and feral cats. The individual who contacted us was enthusiastic and excited about the project. We warned her that a project of this magnitude could take a year or longer and she eagerly agreed to be our ally on the project. We made plans to meet at the barns of the horse track once a week to gather a new batch of cats who we would then take in for spay and neuter surgeries. In addition to the surgeries we provided food to those who set out daily food and water for the cats. When we discovered friendly cats who wished to be indoors, we brought them into our rescue/adoption program to ultimately found forever homes for each of them. The feral cats were returned to the barns to live happy healthy lives. The project was going smoothly, although admittedly a project of this enormity comes with endless hard work. We (co-founders) went to the track 4 or 5 days a week to trap cats and take them back and forth from their veterinary appointments (and then return them after recovery). We met with the individual who contacted us out of concern for these very cats once a week...*for two weeks* and then she disappeared. She was burnt out. At first her calls were filled with excuses and eventually she just stopped responding. No longer did she meet to help us catch and transport the cats. The individual who had been so excited to embark on the project had seemingly fallen off the face of the earth. What were we to do? We had to forge on. It was just the two of us at the time *and countless cats–* at one of many feral cat projects we were working on.

During another feral cat project, we asked the individuals who contacted us for assistance with a rampant feral cat issue in their neighborhood, to become the colony caretakers. We worked daily to trap, neuter and relocate the many feral cats who were in harm's way in their area. Neighbors were chasing, shooting at and kicking the cats. At the start of the project, as we always do, we advised those who contacted us that it would take us working together and likely the project would take 6-months or longer. The two individuals texted us daily for the first four weeks and then disappeared. We had worked around the clock to successfully trap and relocate all but two remaining cats in the colony. There were only two remaining cats and we asked the colony caretakers to set the traps each day and contact us to report back daily. We stressed the importance of catching the last two, so additional kittens would not arrive in the spring.

They set the trap for two days and then stopped. They contacted us from time to time telling us why they were too busy to set the trap or to check the trap. Therefore we scheduled extra time in our day to drive to that location and set and check the traps ourselves. After another week, the individuals stopped contacting us and stopped setting out the traps. Once again, we were on our own to finish the job.

We've had cheerleaders of our organization who get excited about the work that we do and in the light of that excitement they jump on CraigsList or FreeCycle and find pets in need and start taking them in themselves. They tell those that they are taking the animals from that they are "with" our organization. However, they are not approved volunteer foster homes, but they do follow us on Facebook. The individuals take in pet after pet and then contact us at Advocates 4 Animals to say that they got in over their heads and they suddenly need help- their rescue pets need rescued. They say they cannot afford to spay and neuter the pets they saved, they say they cannot afford to feed the pets or that their spouse is angry and the pets are going to be dumped or go to the local pound (a high-kill shelter) that night if we can't take the pets off their hands. While these individuals may have good intentions, they have a lack of a plan and the animals they "rescued" begin going without and can then find themselves stuck facing near certain death at the local pound. The burden is then placed on our organization to clean up the mess, or else know that the pets will be destroyed.

We've had individuals research to locate one of our veterinarians work offices and walk in with their own pet and say that they are a volunteer with Advocates 4 Animals – "just put it on their bill" they are quick to say. Thankfully we have established a strong relationship with our veterinarians and they know who in our organization is authorized to bring in pets and add services to our bill. There are many well-intentioned individuals and cheerleaders who are quick to say "go, go, go!" but are not willing to back what they are applauding. Ultimately, the responsibility is on your shoulders as a director of your organization. If a volunteer on a project falls through, it's up to you to pick up the pieces. If a foster home suddenly calls it quits, it's up to you to secure a new qualified foster home, pronto. It's a heavy daily burden to carry with you and can often be overwhelming.

Wistfully, death is an all too common aspect of animal rescue. And when you're responsible for a high volume of animals in your organization, it can be difficult to find time to grieve the loss of your pet or foster pet. When my senior dog passed away in my arms I was beyond distraught. I wanted to curl up in a ball and stay there for weeks. My eyes were swollen and my heart heavy. But there were questions to answer from foster homes, appointments with potential adopters of pets in our organization and my own foster pets to care for. I took a few hours in the afternoon to hike through the woods and be with my thoughts and then it was time to return to work. I miss my dog dearly and have a framed photo of her next to my computer. I adopted her as a senior dog after she had a tough life in a puppy mill. We only had 3 years together, but I remind myself of how grateful I am to have known her. She helped me in more ways that I can ever adequately articulate. As I move forward and carry her memory close to my heart, I use her life, our bond, as fuel to continue saving other lives in need.

When you're juggling your relationship/family/ household, your day job, your own pets and foster pets and operating an animal rescue it is an exhilarating experience and one not to be taken lightly. But it's important to remind yourself every day, why you're doing what you're doing. It's equally as important to be passionate about your work. If you are experiencing symptoms of Compassion Fatigue, develop realistic ways to combat this listlessness. Maybe taking time to do 20-30 minutes of yoga or meditation each morning will help you ease into your day. Try taking a walk after lunch. This can reduce stress levels and help ease your symptoms. Find what works for you and work it into your daily routine. This is true whether you operate an animal rescue or not. Taking a few minutes for yourself each day can do wonders for yourself and those around you.

Simply taking a few moments to recall (or share with a friend) a few of your favorite rescue moments or adoptions can change the trajectory of your outlook and lift your current disposition. Do your best to keep your focus on the animals you have helped. You know the saying, *"Energy goes where attention flows."* It's true.

At Advocates 4 Animals, and with every active animal rescue organization, we need allies to sustain such a high volume of work. We need supporters who donate and volunteers who stick to their commitments. You won't find these wonderful individuals overnight, but if you persist in your endeavor and if you keep working hard toward your goal of making a difference, the right people will come your way.

Compassion Fatigue is a serious topic and one that needs to be addressed in every organization. Finding ways that you can work to prevent Compassion Fatigue, as well as finding methods of coping with Compassion Fatigue when it strikes, are essential to you and the health of your organization.

CHAPTER 16 CHALLENGE

- Have you previously experienced Compassion Fatigue? What are your signs and symptoms? What helped you recover?

- How will you handle your operations and day to day work when you notice signs of Compassion Fatigue in yourself or your volunteers/ employees? What precautions can you take?

- If/when Compassion Fatigue impacts you, what things can you do to recharge and revitalize yourself at that time?

- If you plan to take a one week vacation annually, how will you continue to operate your organization at that time? What happens if an animal in your organization needs to see the veterinarian or needs emergency care; can someone else authorize these services? Who will check your e-mails and answer phone calls?

Who will keep your website and social media services up to date? If you have a building/ facility, who will hold down the fort while you are on vacation? These are important aspects to consider prior to starting an organization.

OPERATING A FOR PURPOSE BUSINESS

———————

YOU WEAR A LOT OF HATS when operating any non-profit (i.e. for purpose) business! When you operate an animal rescue, you find yourself playing many roles including, but certainly not limited to, rescuing, transport driver, consulting with your veterinarians (most likely on a daily basis), foster parent, pet-sitter, grant writer, fundraiser developer, advertiser, motivator, recruiter, and more. It's easy to get swept away in all of the work (or buried under the mounds of paperwork required to keep a viable organization operating and in the black). Focus and work ethic are essential to your longevity. It may go without saying, but presentation matters too. How you present yourself to your adopters, donors and others matters. Professionalism matters because you are operating a business.

Setting goals and realistic expectations (i.e. intake numbers, adoption rates) while allowing for flexibility and unpredictability are a must in this business. Know what your organization and your staff/volunteers can handle; understand your limits and have a plan for oddities (i.e. returns, behavior issues, large rescues, volunteer drop-out). Your organization's long-term success should equal a win for the animals in your community. Keep the focus on your mission and do the work that you set out to do. Remind yourself every day that you are doing this to save lives. Whether you are an individual wanting to help feral cats in your own neighborhood through TNR(M), someone who is considering starting an animal rescue organization or you are an existing animal rescue agency- your work matters. Every life you save, spay/neuter and adopt matters.

The need for animal rescue organizations is great. Alley Cat Allies reports that 70% of shelter cats are needless killed. Nearly 100% of feral, shy, ill, and injured cats are killed. Shelter death is the number one cause of death in cats; more than any other disease. Artist Mark Barone has painted 5,500 shelter dogs – the number killed in U.S. shelters *each day*. The need is there. Animal rescue is needed. Foster homes are needed. Committed adopters are needed. Leaders are needed. Professionalism is needed. Statistics are needed. Sharing stories with the public about the need for animal rescue and adoption are needed. Collaborations between pounds/shelters and rescue organizations are needed. So much is needed and you – your voice and your actions – can make a difference for lives in need.

CHAPTER 17 CHALLENGE

- What are your short and long-term goals to help animals in need?

- Take time to sketch out your vision. Whether you are an individual or an organization, what do you hope to achieve and how to do see yourself getting there? The more detailed your notes are, the better prepared you will be for the journey ahead.

EPILOGUE

———————

WHETHER YOU ARE an individual active in assisting animals in need or an animal welfare organization (start-up or existing); we can all make a difference right now. No one can tell you exactly how to create a non-profit (i.e. for purpose) business and a life that you love and one that helps others. Our hope is that you will take away bits and pieces from our experiences shared with you throughout the book, to assist you in helping additional animals in need where you live.

It takes us all working together. As someone willing to take a positive action to help animals, you are a leader, an educator and an innovator. You are a role model for others who may be interested in assisting animals in need too. Our words and our actions impact others far and wide. Often we do not realize their full repercussions. We have received letters and e-mails from around the world explaining how reading about our work inspired someone to take action in their own community and to save lives. Those e-mails and letters are always dear to our hearts.

Across the globe additional animal rescue/ adoption, spay/neuter program and pet food pantry programs are urgently needed. One of the most popular questions we are asked is "How can I start a rescue?" It's not a simple one-word answer. If you do it right, if you are actively helping animals in need it may look *easy* to those on the outside. But as with anything worth doing, the endeavor of creating a non-profit (i.e. for purpose) animal welfare organization is filled with endless hard work, dedication, compassion and perhaps, most importantly, a strong business sense. While the need for helping animals is ever- present, the need for creating a viable, sustainable organization is essential. Whether you wish to help one or two animals a year through fostering *for* an organization, or you hope to start your own organization, we applaud you for your efforts. The animals need you! Although everyone's journey will be unique, we can promise you one thing; if you devote even a portion of your life to helping animals in need, you will, at times be blissfully covered in pet fur.

UPDATE

———————

At Advocates 4 Animals we continue to grow our viable programs: spay/neuter, rescue/adoption, TNRM (feral cats/community cats), seniors to seniors and our pet food pantry- to keep pets from ever entering the shelter and facing such terrible odds and harsh circumstances. A positive change in the local pound will take place if and when a compassionate and motivated director is hired at the facility.

In the meantime, we continue to offer our assistance and grow our flourishing programs to lower the number of pets entering the local pound, and therefore significantly lowering the number of unnecessary daily deaths. We continue to discuss the issue with City Council members as we are willing to work together to provide local shelter reform. With shelter killing being the number one cause of death for cats in the United States (more than any disease), we won't give up on our pursuit to advocate and take action for much-needed shelter reform. Rescue Proud Magazine reports in New Hampshire that spay and neuter programs are making a positive impact, helping to keep animals from ever entering the shelter system and therefore saving thousands of innocent lives. In 1993 New Hampshire shelters killed 11,494 pets. When a non-profit organization called STOP (Solutions to Overpopulation of Pets) collaborated with the state's veterinary community everything changed for the animals. Through legislation, STOP spearheaded a state funded spay/neuter program for residents on fixed incomes. The statewide program is funded by a $2 surcharge on all dog license fees. "The money goes into a fund that provides subsidies for sterilizing the pets of low-income families, enabling the pet owners to pay for the surgeries at a fraction of the cost." Within one month of the programs start, 30% fewer animals were euthanized in New Hampshire shelters.

Remember, in 1993 New Hampshire shelters killed 11,494 innocent pets. By 2013 that number was reduced to 1,153. And what's even better? Since 2000 no healthy cats or dogs have been euthanized in New Hampshire shelters.

We would love to see this same progress in every state on the map. It takes relentless work, intelligent leadership and an unwavering commitment to the goal. It's about passion, compassion and hard work: all of which we continue to give to this endeavor every single day at Advocates 4 Animals.

With your support and your continued efforts on this front (no action is ever too small) we can save lives city-by-city, county-by-county and state-by-state. We can reform the outdated shelter system that sadly plagues our country killing more than 3 to 4 million healthy pets every year. Together we can make a lasting stamp on history by insisting on change, insisting on humane education, insisting on compassionate shelter directors and by supporting the local 501(c)3 rescue and spay/neuter organizations who are doing the daily work...we can be the change we wish to see in the world and in doing so, innumerable lives can and will be saved.

Did you enjoy this book?

Please share your thoughts in an *OnlineReview* with your book retailer.

We are so grateful for your support!

Learn more and sign up for FREE book giveaways at: www.StaceyRitzBooks.com or www.StaceysBookBlog.com

Are you starting your own rescue organization?

We hope you've found this book helpful as you pursue your endeavors! While everyone's journey to opening and operating an animal rescue or animal welfare organization is unique, it is our hope that through sharing our experiences with you here, that you will smoothly navigate your way to running a viable organization to help animals in need in your area. Once your organization is up and running, please contact us to share your website. You may win a chance to be featured on the Advocates 4 Animals blog which can help in directing additional supporters to your new organization. Congrats and best of luck!

http://www.advocates4animals.com/contact/

Be sure to check out our additional resources at the end of this book!

DISCLAIMER

The stories and views presented in this book are solely those of its authors. The authors of this book are not lawyers or veterinarians. We are not providing any legal, financial or medical advice in this book. For any specific questions, please contact a licensed lawyer or veterinarian.

About Advocates 4 Animals

"I wondered why somebody didn't do something. Then I realized, I am somebody." –Author Unknown

Advocates 4 Animals is a true labor of love, providing life-saving assistance to pets in need since 2003. Unlike traditional shelter systems, Advocates 4 Animals houses adoptable pets in home environments as opposed to the solitary steel cages typically found in local shelters/pounds. While living in their volunteer foster homes, animals are provided the emotional/social support needed for proper rehabilitation prior to adoption.

About Advocates 4 Animals

With shelter euthanasia being the number one killer of companion animals in the United States, we can all take action to make a difference today. In order to eliminate shelter killing and create No-Kill communities around the world, we must understand that no action is too small. Let's continue working together to reform the system and save lives.

Save a Life: Donate Today

Please consider making a donation to *Advocates 4 Animals* today. No amount is too small and every dollar goes directly to help pets in need. Donations can be made online or via mail.

www.Advocates4Animals.com

Advocates 4 Animals

PO Box 13 Xenia, OH 45385

About the Authors

Stacey Ritz and Amy Beatty spent years volunteering in numerous shelters/pounds and working in kennels and veterinary hospitals prior to founding Advocates 4 Animals. It was while walking city shelter dogs down a gravel alley that the pair decided to officially open Advocates 4 Animals. Understanding the overwhelming amount of animals in need of assistance, Beatty and Ritz began their journey, forging their own unique path.

Leaders in the No Kill Movement, Beatty and Ritz work tirelessly to educate, promote and inspire animal shelters, county pounds and communities to embrace life-saving, humane techniques of rescuing, rehabilitating, altering and ultimately adopting pets into well-matched forever homes.

Books by Stacey Ritz

*Pawsitive Connection: Heartwarming Stories of Animals
Finding People When We Need Them Most*

Cat Connection: Heartwarming Rescue Tales

*Covered in Pet Fur: How to Start an Animal Rescue, The Right
Way*

Letters from Cats: Hilarious & Heartfelt Notes

BOOKS BY STACEY RITZ

Fun(d)raising: 150 Money Making Ideas

Not Your Average Grandma: The Story of a Little Senior Rescue Dog with Big Life Lessons